LEVEL D

STRATEGIES FOR SUCCESS

in Mathematics

STECK-VAUGHN BERRENT PUBLICATIONS

Richard Crowe, M.A., M.A.T.

Credits

Executive Editor: Karen Bischoff

Senior Editor: Amy Losi

Editorial Development: Fox Run Press

Editors: Debra Tursi
Amy Robbins

Design Manager: Steven Coleman

Electronic Production Artist: Jean-Paul Vest

Design and Layout: Jan Jarvis & Jennifer Coton, *Michael William Printery*

Illustrations: Jack Kershner, *Lancelot Art Studio*

ISBN 0-7398-1051-0

Published by Steck-Vaughn/Berrent Publications, a division of Steck-Vaughn Company.

4 5 6 7 8 9 BP 04

Table of Contents

To the Teacher...

*S*trategies for Success in Mathematics has been carefully developed to assist students in learning and reinforcing the skills they will need to solve problems on mathematics tests. This book provides students with specific test-taking strategies that will give them the extra edge they need to do well in math testing situations.

Unit 1:

The goal of this book is to clarify the process for solving math problems, so that math tests become less intimidating for students. Unit 1 introduces a Four-Step Method of Solving Math Problems and nine Math Thinking/ Problem-Solving Strategies. These techniques will help students work through the problems in the remainder of the book. The way to answer each type of math problem is modeled, so students can see how it is done.

Unit 2:

The new problem-solving exams test five clusters of math skills: Numerical Operations; Measurement and Geometry; Numeration, Patterns, and Functions; Data Analysis; and Algebraic Concepts. In Unit 2, students will answer problems that require them to apply these skills.

This unit is designed so that it can be taught intensively (by skill) or cyclically (by method). The problems are separated by strand, so that if you wish to concentrate on one strand, you can do so in detail. However, if you wish to address content in a spiraled fashion, follow a cyclical approach. To do this, have students complete all Set A problems from Chapters Two through Six. Then have students go back and complete Set B of Chapters Two through Six. Finally, let students complete Set C (Chapter Test) of each chapter. This approach more closely matches that of a testing situation.

Unit 3:

The third unit of Strategies for Success in Mathematics contains two practice tests. These tests will assess how well students have learned the strategies necessary to solve problems and think critically.

Unit 1 Strategies

Introduction

Our society cannot work well if people cannot read, write, or do math. Testing is one way that teachers can find out how well you are learning these skills. It is the way we measure both your success as a learner and our success as teachers.

The materials in this book have been carefully prepared to help you learn the skills you will need to do well on tests. You will become aware of your strengths and weaknesses, and you can practice the skills that give you trouble. Here is a breakdown of what you will find:

You will be introduced to a Four-Step Method of Problem Solving, which you can use to answer every math problem you encounter. You will also discover nine Math Thinking/Problem-Solving Strategies. Each of the nine strategies is thoroughly explained and then followed by one sample problem that is worked out for you and one problem that you can do by yourself.

Once you are familiar with the nine strategies, you can practice them by doing the problems throughout this book.

CHAPTER *One*

Math Thinking Strategies

There are many ways to solve mathematical problems. It is important to know some strategies that you can use. These strategies that you will learn here offer ways for you to approach math problems; they help you to better understand what you need to do.

The first key to solving math problems is to follow the **Four-Step Method.**

The Four-Step Method to Solving Math Problems

1. **Think**   *Think about what the problem requires.*
2. **Choose**   *Choose a strategy.*
3. **Solve**   *Solve the problem.*
4. **Check**   *Check your answer.*

The second key is to learn the **Nine Math Thinking Strategies.** Almost every math problem can be solved with one of these strategies.

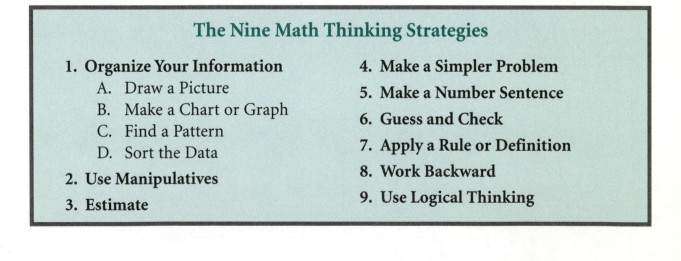

The Nine Math Thinking Strategies

1. **Organize Your Information**
   A. Draw a Picture
   B. Make a Chart or Graph
   C. Find a Pattern
   D. Sort the Data
2. **Use Manipulatives**
3. **Estimate**
4. **Make a Simpler Problem**
5. **Make a Number Sentence**
6. **Guess and Check**
7. **Apply a Rule or Definition**
8. **Work Backward**
9. **Use Logical Thinking**

Throughout the rest of this unit, we'll show you how to use these nine problem-solving strategies.

The chapter is organized as follows:

Chapter Organization

Unit 1 Strategies

1. Organize Your Information ← **Name of Strategy**

B. Make a Chart or Graph ← **Sub-Strategy**

Sometimes, problems are hard to understand because they look complicated. Making a chart or a graph may help you see what is important or see a pattern that helps you solve the problem. → **An explanation of how and when to use the strategy**

Sample Problem

Bryan has a red sweater, a black sweater, and a white sweater. He wants to wear one of them with his Yankees cap, his Indians cap, or his Cardinals cap. Show all the possible combinations Bryan has. → **An example of a problem that calls for this strategy**

10

An explanation of how and when to use the strategy

An example of a problem that calls for this strategy

Unit 1 Strategies

Explanation of Sample Problem

A tree diagram is an organized way to list all the possible combinations when items are being chosen. For Bryan's example, you first draw a tree branch for each of his sweaters. Then, at the end of each sweater branch, you draw a branch for each of his caps. When your tree diagram is finished, you have all nine of Bryan's possible combinations listed.

Red sweater — Yankees cap / Indians cap / Cardinals cap
Black sweater — Yankees cap / Indians cap / Cardinals cap
White sweater — Yankees cap / Indians cap / Cardinals cap

YOUR Turn

A library charges 20 cents for every day that a book is overdue. Lisa's book was due on November 28, but she returned it on December 3. There are 30 days in November. How much did Lisa owe?

A. $0.80
B. $1.00
C. $1.20
D. $1.40

Shows you how you would use the strategy to solve the problem

A problem for you to try

Help with how to answer the Your Turn problem

Organize Your Information: Make a Chart or Graph

STRATEGIES ? to Answer the Problem

Draw a chart to show a calendar from November 28 to December 3 like the one below.

Date	Nov. 28	Nov. 29	Nov. 30	Dec. 1	Dec. 2	Dec. 3
Amount Due						

Then work from left to right to fill in the amount owed each day. By working in an organized way, you can make sure you get a correct answer.

11

1. Organize Your Information

A. Draw a Picture

Sometimes, a math problem seems hard to solve because it contains lots of words. By translating words into pictures, you can often change a problem that looks tough into one that looks familiar.

Sample Problem

Each row in a small theater contains five seats. There are six rows in the theater. How many seats are there in all?

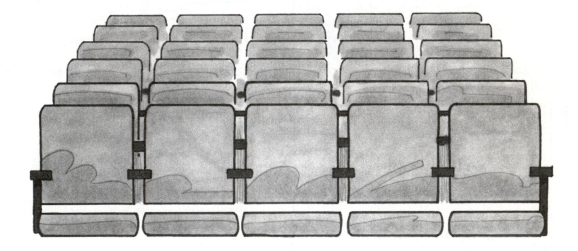

Explanation of Sample Problem

If you use circles to stand for seats, you can turn the problem into a picture.

Study the picture. Counting circles will give you the answer. Or, you may notice that the answer must equal 5 × 6 since the picture shows multiplication. So, there are 5 × 6 = 30 seats in all.

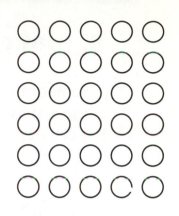

YOUR Turn

There are 19 people waiting to go on a roller coaster. If a car holds 4 people, how many cars are needed for the 19 people?

Organize Your Information: Draw a Picture

STRATEGIES *to Answer the Problem*

Draw a picture to stand for a roller coaster car. Then draw enough copies of the car to fit all 19 people. Remember that only 4 people can fit in a car.

1. Organize Your Information

B. Make a Chart or Graph

Sometimes, problems are hard to understand because they look complicated. Making a chart or a graph may help you see what is important or see a pattern that helps you solve the problem.

Sample Problem

Bryan has a red sweater, a black sweater, and a white sweater. He wants to wear one of them with his Yankees cap, his Indians cap, or his Cardinals cap. Show all the possible combinations Bryan has.

Explanation of Sample Problem

A tree diagram is an organized way to list all the possible combinations when items are being chosen. For Bryan's example, you first draw a tree branch for each of his sweaters. Then, at the end of each sweater branch, you draw a branch for each of his caps. When your tree diagram is finished, you have all nine of Bryan's possible combinations listed.

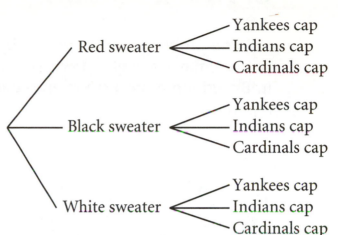

YOUR Turn

A library charges 20 cents for every day that a book is overdue. Lisa's book was due on November 28, but she returned it on December 3. There are 30 days in November. How much did Lisa owe?

A. $0.80

B. $1.00

C. $1.20

D. $1.40

Organize Your Information: Make a Chart or Graph

 **to Answer the Problem**

Draw a chart to show a calendar from November 28 to December 3 like the one below.

Date	Nov. 28	Nov. 29	Nov. 30	Dec. 1	Dec. 2	Dec. 3
Amount Due						

Then work from left to right to fill in the amount owed each day. By working in an organized way, you can make sure you get a correct answer.

1. Organize Your Information

C. Find a Pattern

Some problems can be solved by finding a pattern that repeats. The pattern may be easy to find, or you may have to look very closely to find it. By writing a problem in an organized way, you may help yourself find a pattern.

Sample Problem

A checkerboard looks like the picture below. How many black squares are there on a checkerboard?

Explanation of Sample Problem

You could count all the black squares, or you could look for patterns.

The first pattern you can see is a simple one: since there are 8 rows with 8 squares in each row, the checkerboard represents multiplication. So, there are $8 \times 8 = 64$ squares in all.

The second pattern you can see is that white and black squares take turns appearing on a checkerboard. So, the number of black squares is $64 \div 2 = 32$.

In his first four years in professional baseball, Barry Stock hit 10 home runs, 16 home runs, 22 home runs, and 28 home runs. If Stock continues to increase his home runs in this way, how many would you expect him to hit in his fifth year?

Organize Your Information: Find a Pattern

STRATEGIES
to Answer the Problem

Write Stock's home runs as a list of numbers. By doing this, you can focus on the pattern:

10, 16, 22, 28, ____, …

1. Organize Your Information

D. Sort the Data

When you have to deal with a large number of items, you usually must sort them. Sometimes, sorting means arranging items in order, like the words in a dictionary or the averages on a baseball team. Other times, sorting means counting how often things occur and arranging them into categories.

Once you sort data, problems can be easier to solve.

Sample Problem

One week in April, the high temperatures below were recorded in Framington.

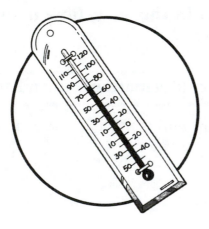

Sunday	48°
Monday	53°
Tuesday	49°
Wednesday	50°
Thursday	44°
Friday	42°
Saturday	39°

What was the median high temperature that week?

Explanation of Sample Problem

The **median** is the middle value in a set of numbers. To find the median, the numbers must be ordered from lowest to highest or from highest to lowest. The temperatures in Framington are ordered as follows:

39°, 42°, 44°, 48°, 49°, 50°, 53°

Since there are 7 temperatures in all, the 4th temperature is the one in the middle: there are 3 temperatures below it and 3 above it. So, the median is 48°.

On a recent test, 20 students received the grades shown below.

A, B, A, C, C, B, A, A, D, C, B, A, A, B, C, D, C, B, A, A

What was the mode of their grades?

STRATEGIES *to Answer the Problem*

Organize Your Information: Sort the Data

There are four different grades. Write each down and then go through the list, making a tally mark for each of the 20 students. The **mode** is the grade that appears most often.

A	
B	
C	
D	

2. Use Manipulatives

When you really want to understand an idea, it helps if you can see it and handle it. Using real objects to understand ideas in math makes you a better problem solver. These objects can be tiles, cubes, blocks, or anything else that helps you.

Sample Problem

The figure below is flipped over the line shown. What will its image look like?

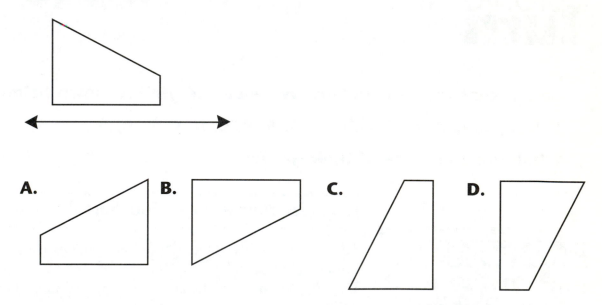

A. **B.** **C.** **D.**

Explanation of Sample Problem

Sometimes you can picture problems like this without drawing anything. But you can also make mistakes that way. Try a hands-on approach instead. Trace the figure and cut it out. Then flip the traced figure over the line to see what its image looks like.

The correct choice is B.

The temperature at 8 A.M. was 72°. By 10 A.M., it had risen 4°. By noon, it had risen 9° more. What was the temperature at noon?

Use Manipulatives
Use a real thermometer or a paper thermometer to model the problem. Start with 72° and work your way through the changes in temperature.

3. Estimate

Sometimes you need an exact answer to a problem, but sometimes you only need an estimate.

When you estimate, you substitute numbers that are easy to work with for numbers that are hard to work with. That usually means rounding numbers and finding ways to make addition, subtraction, multiplication, or division easier. The more you practice estimation, the better you get at it.

Sample Problem

Marisa bought 4 containers of vanilla yogurt for $0.89 each. About how much will they cost in all?

    A.   **$1.00**
    B.   **$2.00**
    C.   **$3.00**
    D.   **$4.00**

Explanation of Sample Problem

The problem asks you to estimate. Since $0.89 is a little less than a dollar, four containers of yogurt will cost about 4 × $1 = $4. The correct choice is D.

Estimate 78 × 106. What two numbers is the product between?
A. 70 and 90
B. 700 and 900
C. 7,000 and 9,000
D. 70,000 and 90,000

Estimate
STRATEGIES to Answer the Problem — Look at the answer choices. The problem is asking you for a rough estimate of the product. Think this way: 78 is close to 80 and 106 is close to 100. Then 80 × 100 can be found without a pencil or calculator.

4. Make a Simpler Problem

When a problem looks difficult, your first thought should be, "*How can I make this easier?*" One way to make a problem easier is to make it smaller. If a problem asks about 10 people or 100 rabbits, change the number to 1, 2, or 3. If a problem involves numbers with decimal places, substitute whole numbers instead. You will find that by making problems simpler, you often figure out exactly how to solve them.

Sample Problem

At last night's concert, 2,348 people attended and 875 of them were students. How many were *not* students?

Explanation of Sample Problem

Sometimes large numbers can distract you. Try simple numbers like 20 and 8 instead:

> At last night's concert, 20 people attended and 8 of them were students. How many were not students?

When the numbers are small, you can *see* the problem better. With numbers like 20 and 8, it is clear that you can find the answer by subtracting: $20 - 8 = 12$. So, the same idea will work for the first problem:

$2,348 - 875 = 1,473$ of those attending the concert were not students.

The sticker on a roast beef at the supermarket is shown below:

<table>
<tr><td colspan="3" align="center">Shop-n-Save</td></tr>
<tr><td>Weight
8.0 lb.</td><td align="center">Price
$30.32</td><td>Price per lb.
$2.79</td></tr>
</table>

Mr. Miller thought $30.32 seemed too high. What should be the price on the sticker?

STRATEGIES ? to Answer the Problem

Make a Simpler Problem

Think of the weight as 8 lbs. and the price per pound as $2. Then you can see that those two numbers should be multiplied to get the price of the roast beef.

5. Make a Number Sentence

In math problems, words and phrases are changed into numbers and symbols such a $+$, $-$, $\times$, and $\div$. Problems then become number sentences that you solve using arithmetic.

Sample Problem

Ariel had $14.25 when she left for work. She spent $4.75 during the day for lunch and a snack. Which number sentence could be used to find how much money she had left at the end of the day?

A. $14.25 + 4.75 = \square$
B. $4.75 - 14.25 = \square$
C. $14.25 - 4.75 = \square$
D. $14.25 \div 4.75 = \square$

Explanation of Sample Problem

Study the words in the problem to figure out what operations are at work. Imagine the problem actually taking place:

- Ariel starts with $14.25.

- Then she takes away $4.75 to buy food. That means subtraction is taking place.

So, the correct choice is C.

YOUR Turn

Mr. Galli had 12 chickens at the beginning of May. He purchased 8 chickens that month and sold 6 chickens in June. Which number sentence could be used to find how many chickens Mr. Galli had at the end of June?

A. $12 + 8 + 6 = \Box$

B. $12 + 8 - 6 = \Box$

C. $12 + 6 - 8 = \Box$

D. $12 - 8 - 6 = \Box$

STRATEGIES *to Answer the Problem*

Make a Number Sentence

Imagine the problem taking place step-by-step. Find a number sentence that represents the amount Mr. Galli has at the end of May before you try to find one for the end of June.

6. Guess and Check

When a problem seems complicated, a good first step is sometimes to guess. Make a guess and then check it by seeing if it solves the problem. If it does, your work is done. If it does not solve the problem, you start all over again with a new guess. Usually, you can improve your second guess by learning something from the first guess.

On a multiple-choice question, remember that only one choice can be correct. Use guess and check when working on difficult problems to help you find choices that cannot be correct.

Sample Problem

**Tommy tells his brother Liam, "I'm twice as old as you."
Liam says, "No, you're not. You're only six years older than me."
It turns out they are both correct. How old are they?**

Explanation of Sample Problem

Start by guessing any age for Liam, and then work through the problem using that number.

If your guess for Liam is 8 years old, Tommy's statement makes his age $2 \times 8 = 16$ years old. But then Liam's statement must be wrong since 16 is 8 more than 8.

So, you make a second guess: suppose Liam is 5 years old. Then Tommy's statement makes him $2 \times 5 = 10$ years old. But, again, Liam's statement must be wrong since 10 is only 5 more than 5.

The first guess makes Tommy's age 8 more than Liam's, and the second guess makes Tommy's age 5 more than Liam's. Next, try a guess between the two. If Liam is 6 years old, then Tommy's statement makes him $2 \times 6 = 12$ years old, which is exactly 6 more than 6. So, both boys are finally correct.

Liam is 6 years old and Tommy is 12 years old.

YOUR Turn

The area of the rectangle shown is 48 square inches. What is the length of the rectangle?

   A. **8 in.**

   B. **10 in.**

   C. **12 in.**

   D. **14 in.**

4 inches

length

Guess and Check

STRATEGIES **to Answer the Problem**

Remember the formula for the area of a rectangle: **Area = length · width.** You can try each of the four answer choices until you find the length that when multiplied by 4 equals 48.

7. Apply a Rule or Definition

In math, you have to learn certain rules and definitions. Many times, when you solve a problem, you must apply a rule or definition before you do any arithmetic. By knowing your rules and definitions well, you will become better at solving math problems.

Sample Problem

Linda measured her height using a tape measure. The tape measure read 54 inches. How tall is Linda in feet and inches?

   A.   **5 ft. 4 in.**

   B.   **5 ft. 6 in.**

   C.   **4 ft. 4 in.**

   D.   **4 ft. 6 in.**

Explanation of Sample Problem

When working with measurements, there are many rules you must remember and apply. For inches, feet, and yards, know these rules:

- 12 inches = 1 foot

- 36 inches = 1 yard

- 3 feet = 1 yard

For Linda's height, use the first rule to convert her height to feet and inches:

Since 12 inches = 1 foot, 4 × 12 inches = 4 × 1 feet. That means that 48 inches = 4 feet. So, Linda's height of 54 inches can be converted:

54 inches = 48 inches + 6 inches

54 inches = 4 feet + 6 inches

54 inches = 4 feet 6 inches

The correct choice is D.

YOUR Turn

Which figure below is a pentagon?

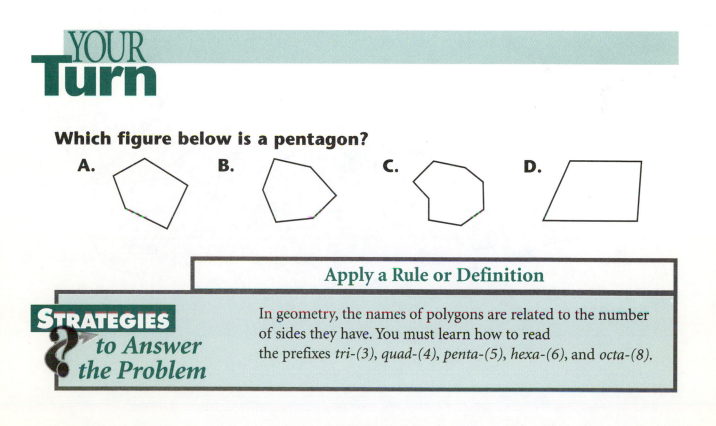

A. B. C. D.

Apply a Rule or Definition

STRATEGIES *to Answer the Problem*

In geometry, the names of polygons are related to the number of sides they have. You must learn how to read the prefixes *tri-(3)*, *quad-(4)*, *penta-(5)*, *hexa-(6)*, and *octa-(8)*.

8. Work Backward

Working backward is a way of solving problems that seem too hard to attack head-on. By working from a later point in a problem back to an earlier point, you can sometimes figure out a solution. On a multiple-choice test, that could mean plugging in the choices, as you learned to do for the strategy of guess and check. In other problems, it means that you rebuild the way a problem started by working from the way it ends.

Sample Problem

The Robinsons left home on a cross-country trip by car. Three days later, they arrived in Chicago. Four days after that, they got to Denver. Three days after that, they reached San Francisco on a Friday. On what day of the week did the Robinsons leave home?

Explanation of Sample Problem

Work backward from the Friday on which they arrived in San Francisco:

- Denver three days earlier – Tuesday

- Chicago four days earlier – Friday

- Home three days earlier – Tuesday

So, the Robinsons left home on a Tuesday.

Maggie left home in the morning and took fifteen minutes to reach school. It took her five more minutes to go to her locker and walk to her classroom. She arrived at her classroom at 8:25. When did Maggie leave for school that morning?

Work Backward
You can work backward from the time Maggie reached her classroom.

STRATEGIES *to Answer the Problem*

9. Use Logical Thinking

Using logical thinking is always a part of doing math. But the strategy of logical thinking is used when you solve a problem by looking at all its possible answers and getting rid of some choices. In that way, you cut down the amount of work you have to do to solve a problem.

For a multiple-choice question, you may be able to show that all but one of the choices are impossible. Then the remaining choice must be the correct one.

Sample Problem

You have 56 cents in nickels and pennies. What is the least number of coins you could have?

A. 4
B. 12
C. 15
D. 16

Explanation of Sample Problem

Use logical thinking to try out possibilities and to eliminate choices.

Choice A is 4 coins. Since 4 nickels are only worth 20 cents, this choice is impossible.

Choice B is 12 coins. If you had 11 nickels and 1 penny, the total value would be:

$$11 \times 5 = \text{ 55 cents in nickels}$$
$$+ 1 \times 1 = \text{ 1 cent in pennies}$$
$$\overline{\text{56 cents}}$$

So, choice B is one way to make 56 cents. And it must be the correct answer since choices C and D use more than 12 coins.

Which number between 50 and 60 is a multiple of both 4 and 7?

A. 84

B. 56

C. 52

D. 28

	Use Logical Thinking
STRATEGIES *to Answer the Problem*	The correct answer must be: 1. between 50 and 60, 2. a multiple of 4, and 3. a multiple of 7. If an answer choice does not fit all three, throw it out! There will only be one choice that fits all three.

Review

The Four-Step Method to Solving Math Problems

1. Think   *Think about what the problem requires.*

2. Choose   *Choose a strategy.*

3. Solve   *Solve the problem.*

4. Check   *Check your answer.*

Review

Math Thinking Strategies

1. Organize Your Information
   A. Draw a Picture
   B. Make a Chart or Graph
   C. Find a Pattern
   D. Sort the Data

2. Use Manipulatives

3. Estimate

4. Make a Simpler Problem

5. Make a Number Sentence

6. Guess and Check

7. Apply a Rule or Definition

8. Work Backward

9. Use Logical Thinking

Unit 2 Instruction

Introduction

Unit 2 consists of five instructional chapters. Each chapter focuses on a specific math cluster: Numerical Operations; Measurement and Geometry; Numeration, Patterns, and Functions; Data Analysis; and Algebraic Concepts.

Each chapter is divided into three sections.

- **Set A: Problems with Strategies**
  Strategies that guide you through the answer process

- **Set B: Practice Problems**
  Problems on which to practice the strategies you've learned

- **Set C: Chapter Test**
  A test on the cluster covered in the chapter

CHAPTER *Two*

Numerical Operations

The phrase *numerical operations* refers to both computation and estimation in problem-solving settings. You can expect to add, subtract, multiply, or divide at any time in this section. Always be certain to read each problem very carefully and to make sure you know exactly what is being asked. Sometimes, when you don't read carefully, you find the correct answer to a problem that wasn't being asked!

Set A: Problems with Strategies

1. Which fraction is smallest?

A. $\frac{1}{2}$　　　B. $\frac{1}{4}$　　　C. $\frac{1}{8}$　　　D. $\frac{3}{8}$

	Use Manipulatives
 **STRATEGIES** *to Answer the Problem*	Use a ruler or fraction bars to represent the numbers. For example, if you divide a bar into four equal sections, one section represents the number $\frac{1}{4}$.

YOUR Turn

Which fraction is equivalent to $\frac{2}{3}$?

A. $\frac{1}{2}$

B. $\frac{3}{4}$

C. $\frac{4}{9}$

D. $\frac{6}{9}$

2. Iris gave 24 stickers to six friends. Each friend got the same number of stickers. How many stickers did each friend get?

    A. 20

    B. 8

    C. 6

    D. 4

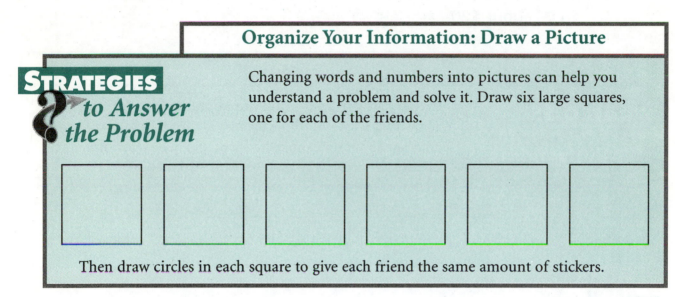

Organize Your Information: Draw a Picture

STRATEGIES *to Answer the Problem*

Changing words and numbers into pictures can help you understand a problem and solve it. Draw six large squares, one for each of the friends.

Then draw circles in each square to give each friend the same amount of stickers.

YOUR Turn

An auditorium has 8 rows with 12 chairs in each row. How many chairs are there in the auditorium?

    A. 20

    B. 86

    C. 96

    D. 816

3. Roger bought a video for $19.99 and a pair of pants for $38.79. If he paid the cashier with a $100 bill, about how much change did Roger receive?

    A.   about $60

    B.   about $40

    C.   about $30

    D.   about $20

Estimate

To estimate his change, you can round the price of the two items Roger bought to the nearest $10. In that way, you can find out about how much he spent and about how much change he received by using mental arithmetic.

Regina spends $3.90 a day traveling to work. She worked 22 days last month. About how much did Regina spend in all traveling to work?

    A. $8

    B. $60

    C. $80

    D. $800

4. Elena walks for exercise daily. On Monday and Tuesday, she walked 3.4 miles each day. On Wednesday, she walked 2.8 miles. How far did she walk on these three days in all?

   A. 9.6 mi.

   B. 8.6 mi.

   C. 6.2 mi.

   D. 5.2 mi.

Write a Number Sentence

STRATEGIES
to Answer the Problem

You can write a number sentence to stand for the problem. Let **n** be the total you are looking for: **n** = Monday's distance + Tuesday's distance + Wednesday's distance. Then fill in the distances to find **n**.

YOUR Turn

Tomas earned $48 working last weekend. He is paid $8 per hour. How many hours did Tomas work?

   A. 40

   B. 8

   C. 7

   D. 6

5. Scott has quarters, dimes, and pennies in his pocket. If he buys an apple that costs 56 cents, what is the fewest number of coins he can use to pay for it?

A. 4

B. 5

C. 8

D. 11

STRATEGIES
? *to Answer the Problem*

Use Logical Thinking

Since the apple costs 56 cents, you know that Scott must use a penny. Then you can figure out how Scott can make 55 cents using the fewest number of quarters and dimes.

YOUR Turn

Find a number between 20 and 80. The number is a multiple of 8. The sum of its digits is 12. What is the number?

6. Diana went out on a Saturday. She spent $1.50 for a bus ride to town, $7.00 for a movie, $5.25 for lunch, and $1.50 for a bus ride home. When she got home, she had $6.25 left. How much money did she have when she left home that morning?

A. $21.50

B. $20.50

C. $20.00

D. $15.25

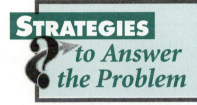

Work Backward

STRATEGIES to Answer the Problem

Picture Diana coming home with $6.25 and imagine working backward to the time she left home that morning. Instead of spending money, imagine Diana taking money back.

YOUR Turn

Chester is thinking of a number. If you add 6 to Chester's number, and divide your sum by 3, you get the number 3. What number is Chester thinking of?

A. 0

B. 1

C. 2

D. 3

7. The students at Danvers School put on a play for three nights. Twice as many people showed up the second night as the first night. Then three times as many people showed up the third night as the first night. In all, 900 people attended the play. How many people attended the first night?

   A.   50

   B.   100

   C.   150

   D.   300

STRATEGIES
to Answer the Problem

Guess and Check

Pick any of the four choices and let it serve as your guess. Then check to see whether it fits the problem sentence-by-sentence. If it does, then you have your solution. If it does not fit any part of the problem, start over again with another choice.

YOUR Turn

A class has 26 students. There are 4 more girls than boys in the class. How many girls are there in the class?

   A.   17

   B.   15

   C.   11

   D.   9

8. Rassa has $18.50 in quarters. How many quarters does she have?

    A. 42

    B. 54

    C. 72

    D. 74

Solve a Simpler Problem

STRATEGIES
to Answer
the Problem

When a problem seems difficult because of the numbers involved, substituting simpler numbers may help you figure out how to solve it. Instead of $18.50 in quarters figure out how many quarters there are in 50 cents, then in $8.00, and finally in $10.00.

YOUR Turn

The population of a town was 5,846 in 1989 and 7,303 in 1999. How many more people lived in this town in 1999 than in 1998?

    A. 1,457

    B. 1,557

    C. 1,657

    D. 1,663

9. Ms. Guzi brought 12 plants to school. Of these, $\frac{1}{3}$ were cactus plants. How many cactus plants did Ms. Guzi bring to school.

    A. 1

    B. 2

    C. 3

    D. 4

Organize Your Information: Draw a Picture

STRATEGIES
*to Answer
the Problem*

You can use circles, squares, or any other shape to stand for each plant. By drawing 12 figures, you can show the 12 plants Ms. Guzi brought to school. Then think: what does $\frac{1}{3}$ mean and how can you show $\frac{1}{3}$ of the 12 plants?

YOUR Turn

Starting at her school, Georgia walked 4 blocks east, then 5 blocks north, then 3 blocks west, and then 6 blocks south. Where was Georgia when she finished walking?

    A. 1 block east and 1 block south of her school

    B. 1 block east and 1 block north of her school

    C. 1 block west and 1 block south of her school

    D. 1 block west and 1 block north of her school

Set B: Practice Problems
Enhanced Multiple-Choice

1. Amy ran a race in 26.72 seconds, Brigit ran the race in 26.9 seconds, and Chris ran the race in 26.48 seconds. How are the three runners ordered from fastest time to slowest time?
   A. Amy, Brigit, Chris
   B. Brigit, Amy, Chris
   C. Chris, Brigit, Amy
   D. Chris, Amy, Brigit

2. Eighteen students collected $3,965 to help support a local homeless shelter. About how much did each student collect, on average?
   A. $20
   B. $200
   C. $400
   D. $2,000

3. Carlo can read 2 pages every 3 minutes. How many pages can he read in 12 minutes?
   A. 8
   B. 9
   C. 10
   D. 11

4. A number between 40 and 70 is a multiple of 6. It is also a multiple of 5. What is the number?
   A. 30
   B. 45
   C. 60
   D. 70

5. Which of the following is the best way to estimate 57 × 73?
  A. 50 × 70
  B. 50 × 80
  C. 60 × 70
  D. 60 × 80

6. Naomi is placing 32 photos in an album. Each page holds 4 photos. How many pages will Naomi use for her photos?
  A. 7
  B. 8
  C. 9
  D. 28

7. How many numbers between 10 and 40 have no remainder when divided by 9?
  A. 1
  B. 2
  C. 3
  D. 4

8. The price of a local bus ride in Kingston from 1995-1999 is shown below. Between which two years did the price of a bus ride increase by the greatest amount?

Year	Price of a Bus Ride
1995	$1.00
1996	$1.50
1997	$1.75
1998	$2.15
1999	$2.25

  A. 1995 and 1996
  B. 1996 and 1997
  C. 1997 and 1998
  D. 1998 and 1999

Open-Ended Problems

9. Quentin has $75. He wants to give his friend $\frac{1}{3}$ of the money. Explain how Quentin can figure out how much to give his friend.

10. Find two different ways to make $1.00 using six coins.

11. The students in the table below are going on a school trip. A bus can hold 30 students. How many buses should be hired?

Grade	Number of Students
4	68
5	63
6	75

12. Find the largest six-digit number that contains the digits 1, 3, 5, 7, 9, and 0, and has a 7 in its hundreds place.

Set C: Chapter Test

Enhanced Multiple-Choice

1. When the Red Devils played the Argonauts in hockey, 22 goals were scored. The Red Devils scored six more goals than the Argonauts. How many goals did the Argonauts score?

   A. 5

   B. 8

   C. 14

   D. 17

2. How many eggs are there in 10 dozen eggs?

   A. 22

   B. 100

   C. 120

   D. 200

3. 480 students are going on a school trip. Each bus can hold 40 students. Which number sentence can be used to find the number of buses needed for the school trip?

   A. $480 + 40 = n$

   B. $480 - 40 = n$

   C. $480 \times 40 = n$

   D. $480 \div 40 = n$

4. Kevin ran $\frac{1}{4}$ mile on Monday, $\frac{3}{4}$ mile on Wednesday, and $1\frac{1}{4}$ miles on Friday. How many miles did he run in all on those three days?

   A. $1\frac{5}{12}$

   B. $1\frac{3}{4}$

   C. 2

   D. $2\frac{1}{4}$

5. Which means the same as (16 × 29) × 42?

    A.   16 × (29 × 42)

    B.   (16 + 29) + 42

    C.   (16 × 29) + (16 × 42)

    D.   (16 × 29) × (16 × 42)

6. Jaime bought two tee shirts that cost $4.89 each and a hat that cost $3.25. About how much did Jaime spend in all?

    A. $7

    B. $9

    C. $11

    D. $13

7. How many different ways are there to make 50 cents using both dimes and nickels?

    A.   3

    B.   4

    C.   5

    D.   6

8. What fraction of the circles are shaded?

    A. $\frac{1}{2}$

    B. $\frac{1}{3}$

    C. $\frac{1}{4}$

    D. $\frac{1}{6}$

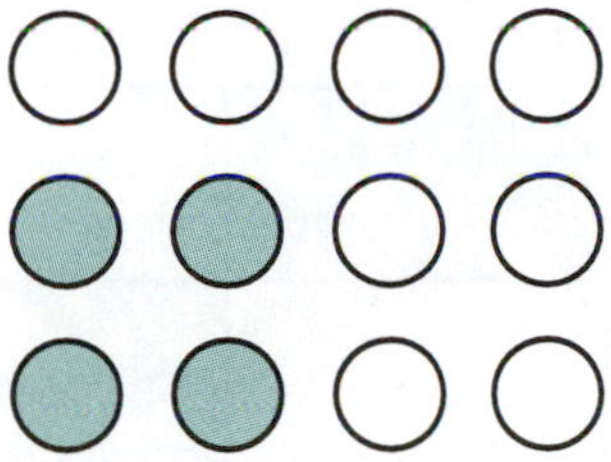

Open-Ended Problems

9. Explain how you compare decimal numbers. Then use your method to order the scores in the table below from greatest to least.

Player	Score
Aaron	86.3
Jake	90.02
Laurene	86.271
Kiera	86.40

10. A student said, "Since 3 is smaller than 4, $\frac{1}{3}$ is smaller than $\frac{1}{4}$." Do you agree or disagree? Explain your reasoning.

11. Explain how you would estimate the product 58×113.

12. Find three equivalent ways to express the fraction of the square below that is shaded.

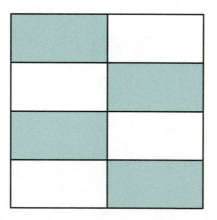

CHAPTER *Three*

Measurement and Geometry

This chapter reviews what you know about shapes and ways to measure. Whenever you do work in geometry and measurement, it is important to make sure you understand the vocabulary terms being used. Before beginning, go over what you know about geometry and measurement.

Set A: Problems with Strategies

1. Burton went to the movies. The movie started at the time shown on the first clock. The movie ended at the time shown on the second clock. How long was the movie?

   A. 2 hr. 25 min.   C. 3 hr. 25 min.
   B. 2 hr. 35 min.   D. 3 hr. 35 min.

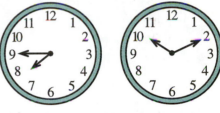

Use Manipulatives

STRATEGIES *to Answer the Problem*

You can use a paper clock or the drawing of the clocks above to count forward from the time the movie starts to the time the movie ends.

YOUR Turn

Yolanda left her home at 7:00. She arrived at work 25 minutes later. Then she spent 45 minutes preparing a spreadsheet. What time was it when Yolanda finished her spreadsheet?

   A. 7:10   B. 8:05   C. 8:10   D. 8:20

2. Which angle is obtuse?

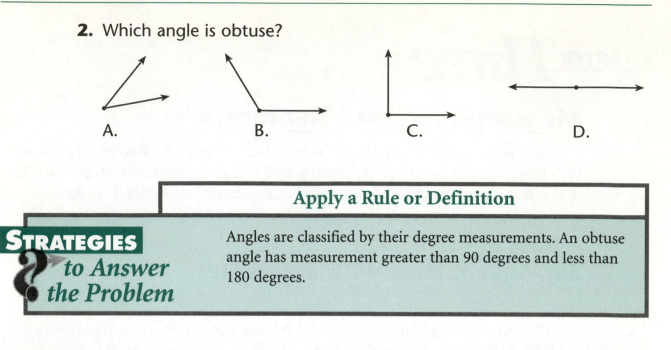

A.   B.   C.   D.

STRATEGIES
to Answer the Problem

Apply a Rule or Definition

Angles are classified by their degree measurements. An obtuse angle has measurement greater than 90 degrees and less than 180 degrees.

YOUR Turn

Which figure must contain a right angle?

    A.   parallelogram
    B.   quadrilateral
    C.   rectangle
    D.   trapezoid

3. The temperature at 6 A.M. is shown on the thermometer below.
By noon, the temperature rose 9°F.
What was the temperature at noon?

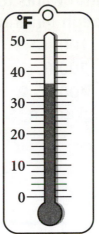

   A. 42°F

   B. 43°F

   C. 45°F

   D. 54°F

Use Manipulatives

STRATEGIES *to Answer the Problem*

Use a paper thermometer to help solve the problem. In the picture shown, numbers are given every 10 degrees. What do the marks between the numbers tell you?

YOUR Turn

The temperature fell 7°F overnight. The temperature was 48°F in the morning.
What was the temperature the night before?

   A. 55°F

   B. 48°F

   C. 45°F

   D. 41°F

4. Martin's field is shaped like a rectangle 60 feet long and 40 feet wide. Martin wants to find the perimeter of the field so that he can buy enough fencing to enclose it. What is the perimeter of Martin's field?

   A. 100 ft.

   B. 200 ft.

   C. 400 ft.

   D. 2,400 ft.

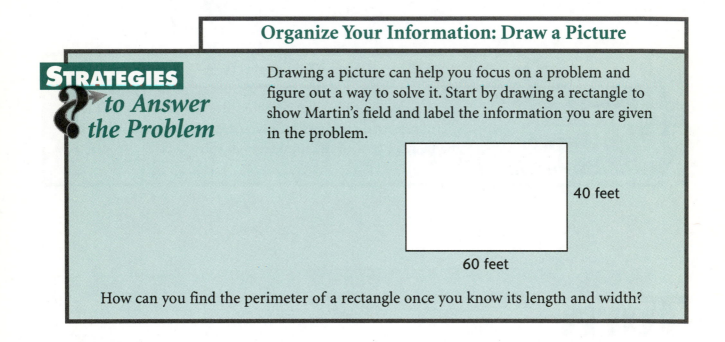

STRATEGIES
? *to Answer the Problem*

Organize Your Information: Draw a Picture

Drawing a picture can help you focus on a problem and figure out a way to solve it. Start by drawing a rectangle to show Martin's field and label the information you are given in the problem.

40 feet

60 feet

How can you find the perimeter of a rectangle once you know its length and width?

YOUR Turn

Helene drew two squares. The first square's sides were 2 centimeters long. The second square's sides were 5 centimeters long. How much greater is the area of the second square than the area of the first square?

   A. 25 sq cm

   B. 21 sq cm

   C. 9 sq cm

   D. 3 sq cm

5. How many seconds are there in 1 hour?

    A. 60

    B. 120

    C. 360

    D. 3,600

Organize Your Information: Make a Chart or Graph

You know how seconds are related to minutes and how minutes are related to hours. Write down those relationships in a chart to help you figure out how seconds are related to hours.

How many centimeters are there in 4 kilometers?

    A. 400

    B. 40,000

    C. 400,000

    D. 4,000,000

6. Three students measured the width of a window in their homes. Hee Sun's window was 1 yard wide. Dan's window was 31 inches wide. Juan's window was 2 feet 9 inches wide. In what order would you list the students, from widest window to the least wide window?

A. Hee Sun, Juan, Dan

B. Hee Sun, Dan, Juan

C. Dan, Juan, Hee Sun

D. Dan, Hee Sun, Juan

STRATEGIES *to Answer the Problem*

Organize Your Information: Sort the Data

Building a table will help you organize your approach. Then you need to find a way to compare the different methods of measuring that the three students used. One way to do this is to change all measurements to inches.

YOUR Turn

Darren's car holds 5 quarts of motor oil. Flavia's car holds 1 gallon of motor oil. Han's car holds 16 cups of motor oil. Trisha's car holds 9 pints of motor oil. Who drives the car that holds the most motor oil?

A. Darren

B. Flavia

C. Han

D. Trisha

7. Reggie drew a square on a coordinate grid. The square had three corners at the points (3, 6), (3, 2), and (7, 2). At which point is the fourth corner of the square?

A. (3, 7)

B. (6, 3)

C. (6, 7)

D. (7, 6)

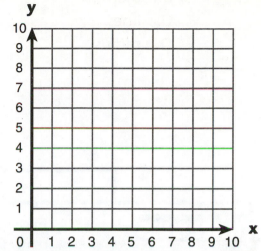

Organize Your Information:
Make a Graph/Use Logical Thinking

STRATEGIES
to Answer the Problem

You can use a graph to organize the information given in the problem. After locating the three corners, try to picture where the fourth corner should go. Remember that the figure must be a square.

YOUR Turn

Which figure must contain parallel sides?

A. triangle

B. trapezoid

C. pentagon

D. circle

8. The circle below has its center at point C. What is $\overline{AB}$ called?

A. circumference

B. diameter

C. line

D. radius

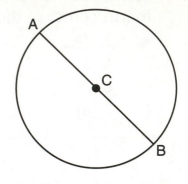

Apply a Rule or Definition

In geometry, there are many definitions that you need to remember. You can help yourself by picturing definitions instead of just trying to remember the words.

YOUR Turn

What is $\overline{AC}$ called in the circle above?

A. circumference

B. diameter

C. line

D. radius

9. What figure will come next in the pattern below?

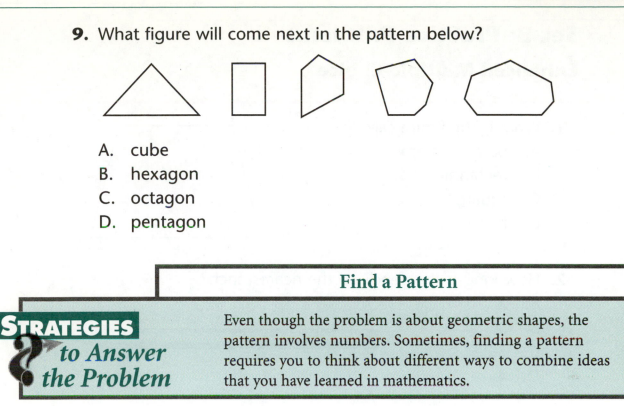

   A. cube

   B. hexagon

   C. octagon

   D. pentagon

Find a Pattern

STRATEGIES
to Answer the Problem

Even though the problem is about geometric shapes, the pattern involves numbers. Sometimes, finding a pattern requires you to think about different ways to combine ideas that you have learned in mathematics.

YOUR Turn

Which shape comes next in the pattern?

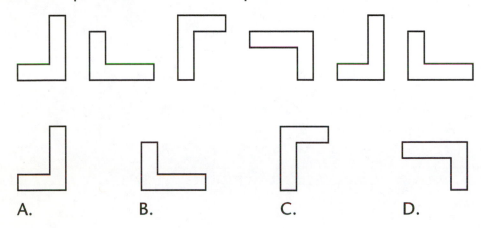

  A.   B.   C.   D.

Set B: Practice Problems

Enhanced Multiple-Choice

1. What is the figure called?
   A. parallelogram
   B. rectangle
   C. square
   D. trapezoid

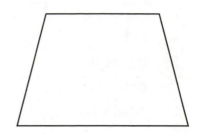

2. How long is the pencil, to the nearest inch?
   A. 2
   B. 3
   C. $3\frac{1}{2}$
   D. 4

3. The sides of a rectangle are 10 centimeters and 6 centimeters long. What is the area of the rectangle?
   A. 16 sq cm
   B. 32 sq cm
   C. 60 sq cm
   D. 120 sq cm

4. What temperature is shown on the thermometer?
   A. 6°C
   B. 10°C
   C. 11°C
   D. 12°C

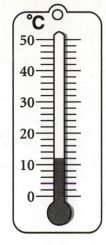

5. How many lines of symmetry does the letter have below?
   A. 0
   B. 1
   C. 2
   D. 4

6. How many faces does the cube have?
   A. 4
   B. 6
   C. 8
   D. 12

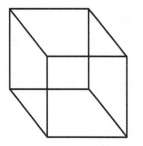

7. Which of the containers below holds the most?

A.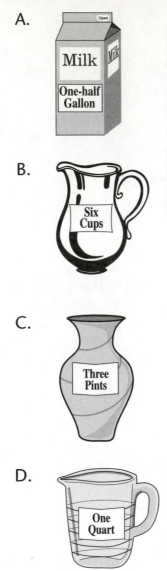

B.

C.

D.

8. What can you conclude about the two triangles below?

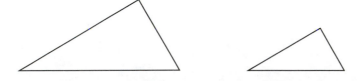

A. The two triangles are both congruent and similar.

B. The two triangles are congruent but not similar.

C. The two triangles are similar but not congruent.

D. The two triangles are neither congruent nor similar.

Open-Ended Problems

9. Use capital letters to draw three letters that have a horizontal line of symmetry and three letters that have a vertical line of symmetry.

10. Estimate the area of the figure shown. Explain your method.

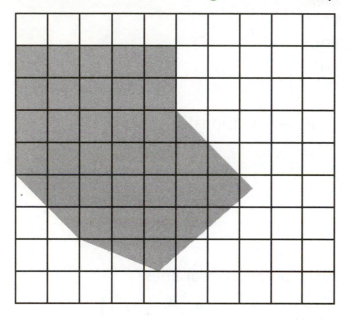

11. Jerome drew a rectangle with a perimeter of 20 feet. Draw four different rectangles that Jerome might have drawn. Label the length and width of each rectangle.

12. Find how many minutes there are in a month containing 30 days.

Set C: Chapter Test
Enhanced Multiple-Choice

1. Deanna arrived at the library at 4:25. She left the library at 6:15. How much time did Deanna spend at the library?
   A. 2 hr. 50 min.
   B. 2 hr. 10 min.
   C. 1 hr. 50 min.
   D. 1 hr. 10 min.

2. Which figure is three-dimensional?
   A. cube
   B. line
   C. square
   D. triangle

3. Which figure shows perpendicular lines?

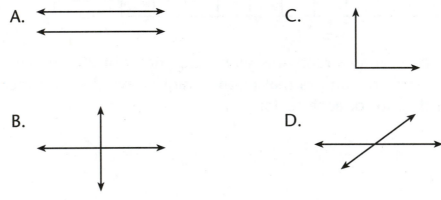

   A.

   B.

   C.

   D.

4. How many millimeters are there in 6 meters?
   A. 60
   B. 600
   C. 1,006
   D. 6,000

5. The calendar for August is shown below. Uncle Ed is coming to visit on the third Wednesday of the month. On what date is Uncle Ed coming?

A. 13

B. 20

C. 21

D. 27

SUN	MON	TUE	WED	THU	FRI	SAT
					1	2
3	4	5	6	7	8	9
10	11	12	13	14	15	16
17	18	19	20	21	22	23
24	25	26	27	28	29	30
31						

August

6. Which letter has a horizontal line of symmetry?

A. **S**   B. **D**   C. **M**   D. **J**

7. The points $A(1, 3)$, $B(2, 5)$, $C(5, 5)$, and $D(4, 3)$ are drawn on a coordinate grid. What type of figure is $ABCD$?

A. parallelogram

B. rectangle

C. square

D. trapezoid

8. Which unit is most appropriate for measuring the weight of a slice of bread?

A. yard

B. ton

C. pound

D. ounce

Open-Ended Problems

9. Explain the differences among acute, right, and obtuse angles, and draw an example of each.

10. Ollie has a set of small cubes that measure 1 inch along each edge. Using his cubes, Ollie formed a large cube measuring 3 inches along each edge. How many cubes did Ollie use?

11. Describe the figure below as fully as you can.

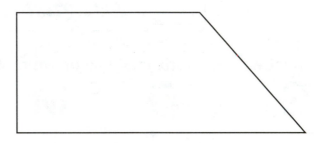

12. A pint of heating oil weighs about 1 pound. An oil tank in a house holds about 300 gallons of oil. Estimate the weight of the oil tank when it is filled with oil.

CHAPTER *Four*

Numeration, Patterns, and Functions

Finding patterns is an important part of problem solving in mathematics. Numbers repeating or shapes changing according to certain rules are two examples of patterns. When you can describe a pattern using a rule, you call the rule a function.

In this chapter, you will solve problems by examining and finding patterns and functions. In addition, the basic concepts of number and numeration will be reviewed.

Set A: Problems with Strategies

1. Tina ran a race in 38.79 seconds. In which place does the digit 9 occur?
   A. tens
   B. hundreds
   C. tenths
   D. hundredths

Organize Your Information: Make a Chart

STRATEGIES *to Answer the Problem*

Draw a place value chart that includes place values to the left of the decimal point and to the right of the decimal point. Label the place values outward from the decimal point and then fill in the number 38.79.

YOUR Turn

Write the number $(3 \times 10{,}000) + (5 \times 1{,}000) + (1 \times 10)$ in standard form.
   A. 35,100   B. 35,010   C. 3,510   D. 351

2. What number is missing from the sequence below?

9, 18, 27, 36, _____, 54

A.   45

B.   46

C.   47

D.   48

STRATEGIES
to Answer the Problem

Organize Your Information: Find a Pattern

To figure out how a sequence works, look for a pattern. Look at the first two numbers to see how they are related. If you have a guess at the pattern, check to see whether it fits the rest of the sequence.

YOUR Turn

Which number is missing from the sequence below?

3, 6, 12, 24, _____, 96

A.   36

B.   48

C.   54

D.   58

3. The table below shows input and output. What rule can you use to convert input to output?

A. subtract 16

B. add 16

C. divide by 5

D. multiply by 5

Input	Output
20	4
25	5
40	8
60	12

Guess and Check

STRATEGIES to Answer the Problem

The rule that you find must be correct for each pair of input and output numbers. You can solve the problem by guessing one of the four choices and seeing if it works for each pair of numbers. If a rule does not work for any pair of numbers, you know that rule is incorrect.

YOUR Turn

What rule is used to go from one number to the next number in the sequence below?

4, 8, 12, 16, 20, ...

A. multiply by 2

B. divide by 2

C. subtract 4

D. add 4

4. Which number below is odd?

    A. 5.5

    B. 3,332

    C. 2,221

    D. 1,000

Apply a Rule or Definition

STRATEGIES to Answer the Problem

You must learn and use many definitions when you do mathematics. You can tell if a whole number is even or odd by looking at the digit in its ones place.

YOUR Turn

Hank Aaron had 3,771 hits in his major league baseball career. How many hits is that, rounded to the nearest hundred?

    A. 4,000

    B. 3,800

    C. 3,770

    D. 3,700

5. Todd has 5 black marbles and 7 white marbles. What fraction of his marbles is black?

- A. $\frac{5}{12}$
- B. $\frac{5}{7}$
- C. $\frac{7}{5}$
- D. $\frac{12}{5}$

Organize Your Information: Draw a Picture

STRATEGIES
*to Answer
the Problem*

Draw a circle for each marble and shade the black ones. Then remember that fractions can be used to represent parts of a whole. What is the whole in this problem? What part are you looking for?

YOUR Turn

Kitty has $0.90 in her pocket. Two of the coins are quarters. The rest of the coins are dimes. What fraction of the coins is quarters?

- A. $\frac{1}{3}$
- B. $\frac{2}{3}$
- C. $\frac{4}{9}$
- D. $\frac{5}{9}$

6. What shape comes next in the pattern below?

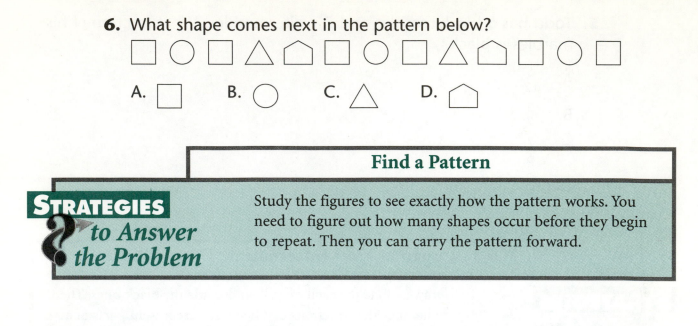

A. ☐ B. ◯ C. △ D. ⌂

Find a Pattern

STRATEGIES ❓ *to Answer the Problem*

Study the figures to see exactly how the pattern works. You need to figure out how many shapes occur before they begin to repeat. Then you can carry the pattern forward.

YOUR Turn

Viata sold 3 magazine subscriptions on Monday this week. She sold 2 more subscriptions on Tuesday than she had on Monday. Then she sold 2 more subscriptions on Wednesday than she had on Tuesday. If this pattern continues every day, how many subscriptions will Viata sell on Monday next week?

A. 13
B. 15
C. 16
D. 17

7. How is the number *three hundred three and three tenths* written in standard form?

    A. 330.3

    B. 303.3

    C. 330.03

    D. 303.03

Organize Your Information: Make a Chart
 **STRATEGIES** *to Answer the Problem*   Read the number again and try to note the place values as you read it. Then draw a place value chart to help you identify the correct way of writing the number in standard form. Fill in the number in the place value chart from left to right as you read it aloud.

YOUR Turn

How is the number 450.017 written in words?

    A. four hundred five and seventeen hundredths

    B. four hundred five and seventeen thousandths

    C. four hundred fifty and seventeen hundredths

    D. four hundred fifty and seventeen thousandths

8. On the first day of gym class, Chaz did 1 push-up. On the second day of gym class, Chaz did 2 push-ups. Then he set a goal. In each gym class, he would try to do as many push-ups as he had done in the last two gym classes combined. If Chaz is able to achieve his goal, how many push-ups will he do in the sixth gym class?

A. 6

B. 12

C. 13

D. 21

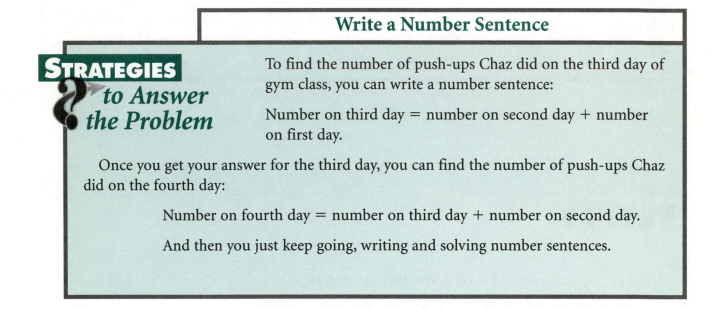

Write a Number Sentence

STRATEGIES
to Answer the Problem

To find the number of push-ups Chaz did on the third day of gym class, you can write a number sentence:

Number on third day = number on second day + number on first day.

Once you get your answer for the third day, you can find the number of push-ups Chaz did on the fourth day:

Number on fourth day = number on third day + number on second day.

And then you just keep going, writing and solving number sentences.

YOUR Turn

The first two numbers in the sequence below are 1 and 3. Each number after those two is found by multiplying the two numbers before it. What will the sixth number in the sequence be?

1, 3, 3, 9, ...

A. 9

B. 27

C. 240

D. 243

9. A pattern using four letters is shown here.

L, O, G, E, L, O, G, E, L, O, ...

What will the 40th letter in the pattern be?

A. L

B. O

C. G

D. E

Solve a Simpler Problem/ Find a Pattern

STRATEGIES *to Answer the Problem*

You can carry out the sequence for all 40 letters, or you can solve a simpler problem. Since the pattern repeats every four letters and $10 \times 4 = 40$, the 40th letter will be the same as the 4th letter.

YOUR Turn

Find the product.

$$40,000 \times 30,000$$

A. 120,000,000

B. 1,200,000,000

C. 12,000,000,000

D. 120,000,000,000

Set B: Practice Problems

Enhanced Multiple-Choice

1. Which number is even?
   A. 3,010
   B. 301
   C. 229
   D. 4.4

2. Which number is missing from the sequence?

   4, 12, 20, 28, _____, 44
   A. 34
   B. 36
   C. 38
   D. 40

3. How many small squares will there be in the fifth figure of the pattern?

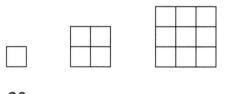

   A. 20
   B. 25
   C. 30
   D. 36

4. What fraction describes the part of the circle that is shaded?

   A. $\frac{1}{2}$

   B. $\frac{1}{1}$

   C. $\frac{6}{3}$

   D. $\frac{3}{3}$

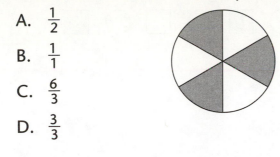

5. How is the number 405.08 written in words?
   A. four hundred five and eight hundredths
   B. four hundred five and eight tenths
   C. four hundred fifty and eight hundredths
   D. four hundred fifty and eight tenths

6. On March 1, 6 people bought tickets to a school play. On March 2, 10 people bought tickets. On March 3, 14 people bought tickets. On March 4, 18 people bought tickets. If this pattern continues, how many people would you expect to buy tickets on March 20?
   A. 78
   B. 80
   C. 82
   D. 84

7. What shape comes next in the geometric pattern?

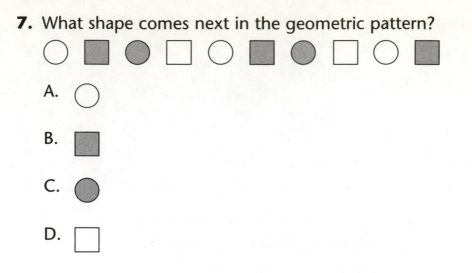

A. ○

B. ■

C. ●

D. □

8. What number is in the thousands place of 56,219.8043

A. 3

B. 4

C. 5

D. 6

Open-Ended Problems

9. Describe the rule that is used to create output from input in the table below. Then find two more pairs of input and output.

Input	Output
16	8
18	10
22	14
30	22

10. Draw a picture to show the fraction $\frac{1}{3}$.

11. The first thousand whole numbers are 1, 2, 3, 4, 5, ... , 999, 1,000. How many of these numbers are even? Explain your reasoning.

12. Create your own rule for a sequence that starts with the number 100 and uses addition or subtraction to find the rest of its numbers. Show your rule and the first six terms of your sequence.

Set C: Chapter Test
Enhanced Multiple-Choice

1. What fraction describes the part of the triangle that is shaded?

A. $\frac{4}{5}$

B. $\frac{4}{9}$

C. $\frac{5}{4}$

D. $\frac{9}{4}$

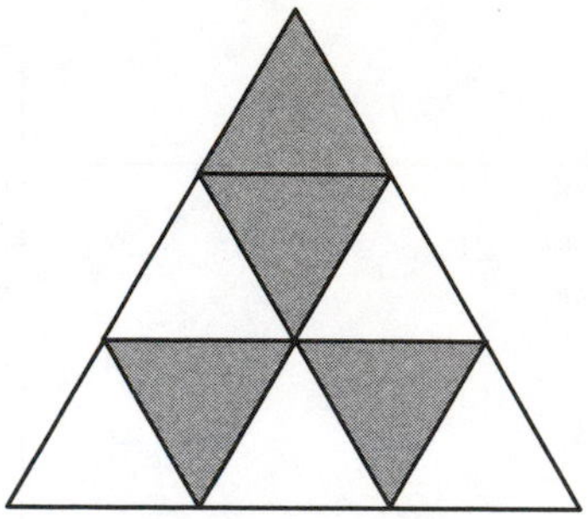

2. The first two numbers in the sequence below are 5 and 10. Each other number is found by adding the two numbers before it. What will the seventh number in the sequence be?

    5, 10, 15, 25, …

A. 55

B. 65

C. 105

D. 170

3. Which statement is **not** true?

A. The sum of two even numbers is an even number.

B. The sum of two odd numbers is an even number.

C. The product of two even numbers is an even number.

D. The product of two odd numbers is an even number.

4. How many squares will be shaded in the next figure of the pattern below?

A. 16

B. 20

C. 25

D. 36

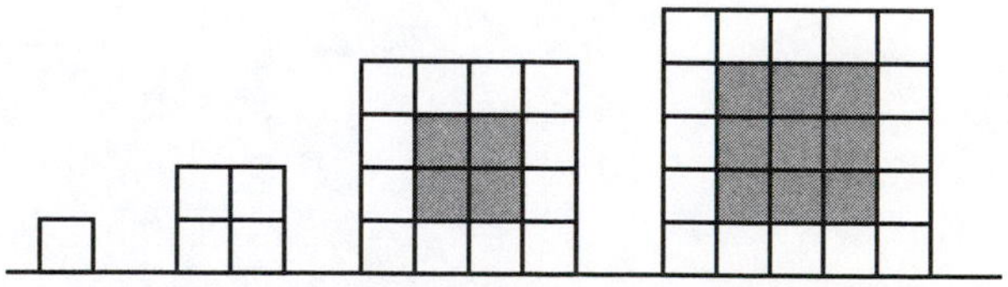

5. How is the number *eight thousand twenty and five tenths* written in standard form?
   A. 820.5
   B. 820.05
   C. 8,020.5
   D. 8,020.05

6. A pattern using five letters is shown here.
   T, R, U, L, Y, T, R, U, L, Y, T, R, ...
   What will the 28th letter in the pattern be?
   A. T
   B. R
   C. U
   D. L

7. How is the number 402,050 written in expanded form?
   A. $(4 \times 100{,}000) + (2 \times 1{,}000) + (5 \times 10)$
   B. $(4 \times 100{,}000) + (2 \times 100) + (5 \times 10)$
   C. $(4 \times 100{,}000) + (2 \times 100) + (5 \times 1)$
   D. $(4 \times 10{,}000) + (2 \times 1{,}000) + (5 \times 10)$

8. The table below shows input and output.
   What rule can you use to convert input to output?
   A. subtract 14
   B. add 14
   C. divide by 3
   D. multiply by 3

Input	Output
7	21
8	24
9	27
10	30
11	33

Open-Ended Problems

9. Design a necklace that contains 48 colored beads. Create a repeating pattern as part of your design. Describe your design and draw your necklace.

10. Create your own rule for a sequence that starts with the number 10 and uses multiplication to find the rest of its numbers. Show your rule and the first six terms of your sequence.

11. Explain what a mixed number is. Give an example of a mixed number in the real world.

12. Explain how to round a four-digit whole number to the nearest hundred.

CHAPTER *Five*

Data Analysis

Watch the evening news or read the morning newspaper, and you are sure to see data. When you look at charts, tables, graphs, or statistics, you need to know how to read and interpret data. When you report ideas of your own in class, you need to know how to summarize and present data. This chapter reviews the many ways you deal with data in daily life.

Set A: Problems with Strategies

1. The 15 students in Mr. Harrigan's class received the scores shown below on a social studies test. What was the median test score?

96, 83, 70, 80, 92, 95, 75, 85, 100, 84, 100, 92, 90, 92, 86

A. 92　　　　B. 90　　　　C. 88　　　　D. 85

STRATEGIES *to Answer the Problem*

Organize Your Information: Sort the Data

The **median** of a set of numbers is the middle number. To find the median, you must first sort the numbers in order from smallest to greatest or from greatest to smallest. In that way, you can find the middle number.

YOUR Turn

What was the mode test score in Mr. Harrigan's class?

A. 92

B. 90

C. 88

D. 85

2. Anita has three hats and four scarves. She wants to wear a different combination of hat and scarf each day. How many different hat and scarf combinations are there?

A. 7

B. 9

C. 10

D. 12

Hat	Scarf
Black	Red
White	White
Blue	Plaid
	Striped

Organize Your Information: Draw a Picture

STRATEGIES to Answer the Problem

When you have to find ways to combine things, tree diagrams can help organize your thinking. By drawing a tree diagram, you can list all the possible combinations. First, draw a branch for each of Anita's hats. Then, at the end of each hat branch, draw a branch for each of Anita's scarves. The result will be a tree diagram in which the number of branches equals the number of combinations Anita can choose from.

YOUR Turn

A movie theater sells plain, caramel, and spicy popcorn in small, medium, and large tubs. If you want to buy popcorn at this movie theater, how many choices do you have?

A. 3

B. 6

C. 9

D. 12

3. The spinner shown below is spun 100 times.
Which number is most likely to be spun the greatest amount of times?

A. 1
B. 2
C. 3
D. 4

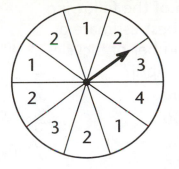

	Use Logical Thinking

to Answer the Problem

When the spinner is spun, it could land on any of the numbers 1, 2, 3, or 4. So, you cannot say for certain which number will be spun the greatest amount of times. But logical thinking helps you predict which number will be spun the most. Look at all the sections of the spinner to see if any number appears more often than the others.

YOUR Turn

A number cube is numbered 1, 2, 3, 4, 5, and 6. The cube is rolled twice. Which of the following is an impossible event?

A. The cube lands on 4 both times it is rolled.
B. The cube lands on an odd number both times it is rolled.
C. The two numbers that the cube lands on have a sum of 12.
D. The two numbers that the cube lands on have a sum of 1.

4. The line graph shows the number of bicycles sold at Robert's Bicycle Shop during the first seven months of the year.

Which of the following is the best estimate of the number of bicycles sold in April?

A. 100

B. 150

C. 200

D. 250

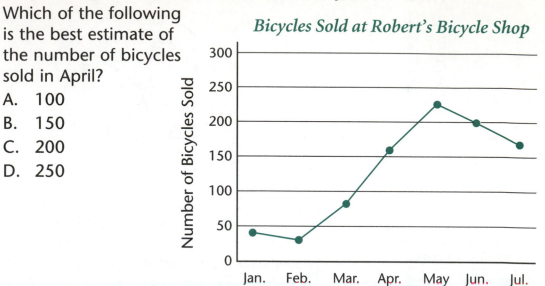

Bicycles Sold at Robert's Bicycle Shop

Estimate

STRATEGIES
to Answer the Problem

When graphs involve large numbers, reading those graphs takes estimation skills. One of the first things you must do when you examine a graph is to look at the scale. The scale on this graph is 50. Understanding the scale allows you to interpret points and estimate values on a graph.

YOUR Turn

In which month were the greatest number of bicycles sold at Robert's Bicycle Shop?

A. April

B. May

C. June

D. July

5. Six students collected books to donate to a children's library.

What was the mean number of books collected by the students?

A. 46

B. 56

C. 58

D. 63

Student	Number of Books
Abbie	56
Bo	60
Aileen	70
Max	45
Crystal	91
Noreen	56

Apply a Rule or Definition/ Write a Number Sentence

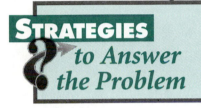

STRATEGIES
to Answer the Problem

The **mean** of a set of values is sometimes called the average. You find it by adding the values together and dividing by the number of values.

YOUR Turn

What was the range of books collected by the students?

A. 46

B. 56

C. 58

D. 63

6. Mrs. Faherty has $30. She wants to buy a dozen roses and three cactus plants as gifts. The table below shows the cost of a dozen roses and the cost of one cactus plant at four different flower shops. At which flower shop will Mrs. Faherty have enough money to buy what she wants?

A. Aster Place

B. Deanna's

C. Flower Folly

D. Greenwood

Flower Shop	Dozen Roses	Cactus
Aster Place	$25	$2
Deanna's	$13	$6
Flower Folly	$20	$10
Greenwood	$15	$4

Guess and Check

STRATEGIES
to Answer the Problem

Start with any of the four possible choices as your guess. Figure out the cost of a dozen roses and three cactus plants at that flower shop. If the cost is $30 or less, your guess is the correct answer. If the cost is more than $30, start over with a new guess. Always be careful to make sure you are figuring out the total cost correctly.

YOUR Turn

Rosemary bought three dozen roses and two cactus plants. Her total cost was $80. At which flower shop did Rosemary shop?

A. Aster Place

B. Deanna's

C. Flower Folly

D. Greenwood

7. A bag contains 14 slips of paper. The letters M, U, L, T, I, P, L, I, C, A, T, I, O, N are written on one slip of paper each. Santhosh reaches into the bag and selects a slip of paper. What is the probability that the slip of paper contains the letter I?

    A. $\frac{3}{14}$

    B. $\frac{1}{14}$

    C. $\frac{1}{13}$

    D. $\frac{1}{10}$

Apply a Rule or Definition

STRATEGIES

to Answer the Problem

When you want to know the probability of some event occurring, you should apply the definition:

$$\text{Probability} = \frac{\text{number of ways the event can occur}}{\text{number of ways all events can occur}}$$

Read the problem carefully to figure out what the numerator and denominator should be. Then you will have your probability.

YOUR Turn

A number cube is numbered 1, 2, 3, 4, 5, and 6. The cube is rolled once. What is the probability that an odd number is rolled?

    A. $\frac{1}{1}$

    B. $\frac{2}{3}$

    C. $\frac{1}{2}$

    D. $\frac{1}{3}$

8. At Lita's job, she spends $\frac{1}{2}$ of her time as a cook, $\frac{1}{3}$ as a manager's assistant, and $\frac{1}{6}$ as a trainer. Which circle graph best shows how Lita spends her time at work?

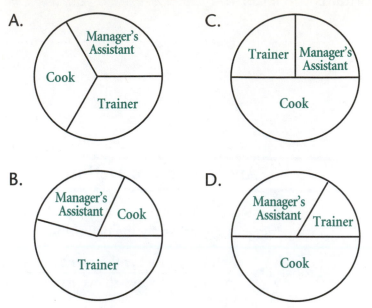

A.
C.
B.
D.

Organize Your Information:
Make a Chart or Graph/Use Logical Thinking

STRATEGIES
*to Answer
the Problem*

Since Lita has three different jobs, the circle graph must have three different sections. But the sections are not equal since she does not divide her time at work equally. The fractions tell you how to divide Lita's circle graph.

YOUR
Turn

Rene wants to show how the price of mailing a letter has increased over the past 40 years. Which method is her best choice?

   A.   circle graph
   B.   line graph
   C.   tree diagram
   D.   Venn diagram

9. Students at the Harrison School were asked to make balloons for an annual town parade. The pictograph shows how many were made by students in four grades. How many balloons were made by Grade 4 students?

A. 5

B. 50

C. 250

D. 300

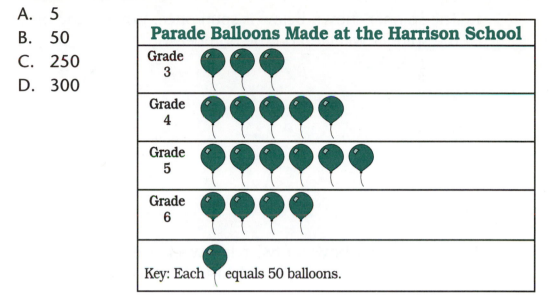

Parade Balloons Made at the Harrison School

Grade 3	
Grade 4	
Grade 5	
Grade 6	

Key: Each ⬤ equals 50 balloons.

Make a Number Sentence

Strategies to Answer the Problem

Read the pictograph carefully to find out what each picture means. Then you can find the number of balloons made in Grade 4 by counting the pictures and writing a number sentence.

YOUR Turn

How many more balloons were made in Grade 5 than in Grade 3?

A. 3

B. 50

C. 100

D. 150

Set B: Practice Problems

Enhanced Multiple-Choice

1. The spinner shown below is spun once. What is the probability that the spinner will land on the number 3?

   A. $\frac{1}{8}$

   B. $\frac{1}{7}$

   C. $\frac{3}{8}$

   D. $\frac{3}{5}$

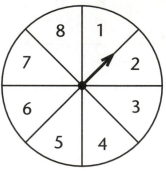

2. Cynthia went bowling twice last week. Her scores were 106, 126, 114, 96, 110, and 114. What was her mean bowling score?

   A. 111

   B. 112

   C. 113

   D. 114

Four students kept track of how many movies they saw one summer. Use their tally chart to answer problems 3 and 4.

Summer Movie Tally Table	
Clive	ЛНТ ///
Judith	ЛНТ //
Pauline	ЛНТ ЛНТ /
Rex	ЛНТ ЛНТ ////

3. Who saw the most movies last summer?

   A. Clive   B. Judith   C. Pauline   D. Rex

4. How many movies did Pauline see last summer?

   A. 9   B. 10   C. 11   D. 15

5. Miller's Fountain serves 4 flavors of ice cream and 3 types of sundae topping. If you want to order ice cream with a topping, how many different combinations are possible?

A. 7   B. 9   C. 12   D. 64

6. A number cube contains the numbers 1, 2, 3, 4, 5, and 6. The number cube is rolled 60 times. About how many times would you expect an even number to be rolled?

A. 40

B. 30

C. 20

D. 10

7. The table below shows the number of boys and girls from four grades who take part in their school's soccer program.

In which grade did the least number of students join the soccer program?

A. 2

B. 3

C. 4

D. 5

Grade	Boys	Girls
2	32	40
3	38	32
4	36	39
5	45	41

8. Tammy likes old movies. She decided to ask other fans of old movies who their favorite silent film stars are. The circle graph below shows what she found out.

Who was the most popular choice among the fans Tammy asked?

A. Charlie Chaplin

B. John Gilbert

C. Buster Keaton

D. Mary Pickford

FAVORITE SILENT FILM STARS

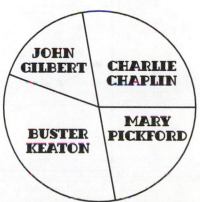

Open-Ended Problems

9. A number cube that comes with board games contains the numbers 1, 2, 3, 4, 5, and 6 on its six faces. Suppose you want to play a board game but you do not have a number cube. Design a spinner that could be used instead of the number cube.

10. Tara took six tests last month and her mean score was 90. On each of those tests, she had a different score. Create a set of six test scores that fit this problem.

11. Twenty students were asked to name their favorite ice cream flavor. The table below shows the results.

    Draw a graph to fit the data.

Flavor	Number of Students
vanilla	6
chocolate	8
strawberry	4
other	2

12. Study the line graph below. Then write three things you learned from it.

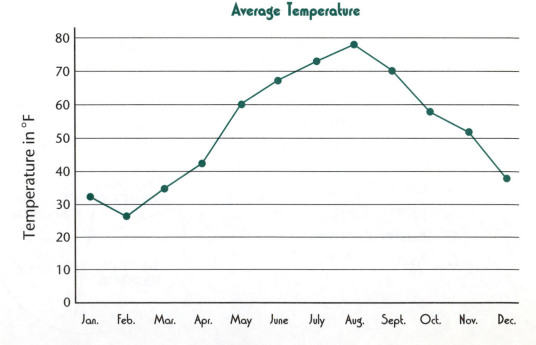

Average Temperature

Set C: Chapter Test
Enhanced Multiple-Choice

The coach of a school basketball team made the bar graph below to show how the team has done over five years. Use the bar graph to answer problems 1-3.

Basketball Victories 1995-1999

1. In which year did the basketball team win its greatest number of games?
   A. 1996   B. 1997   C. 1998   D. 1999

2. How many games did the basketball team win in 1995 and 1996, combined?
   A. 7   B. 11   C. 14   D. 22

3. Over the five-year period, what is the median number of games won by the basketball team?
   A. 8   B. 9.2   C. 10   D. 14

4. The spinner shown below is spun once. Which of the following is a certain event?
   A. The spinner will land on 3.
   B. The spinner will land on 4.
   C. The spinner will land on an even number.
   D. The spinner will land on an odd number.

To help sell tickets to a school band performance, four students wrote and mailed letters to parents. The pictograph shows how many letters each of the four students sent out. Use the pictograph to answer problems 5 and 6.

5. Which student sent out the fewest letters?

    A. Carlo

    B. Kim

    C. Vilma

    D. Wendy

Letters Sent to Parents	
Carlo	✉✉✉
Kim	✉✉✉✉
Vilma	✉✉✉✉✉✉
Wendy	✉✉✉✉✉
Key: Each ✉ equals 100 letters.	

6. How many more letters than Kim did Vilma send out?

    A. 200

    B. 100

    C. 2

    D. 1

7. Suppose you asked 100 people to name a number between 1 and 10. What do you call the number that is named most often by the 100 people?

    A. the mean

    B. the median

    C. the mode

    D. the range

8. A bag contains 9 slips of paper. The letters G, E, O, G, R, A, P, H, Y are written on one slip of paper each. Paul reaches into the bag and selects a slip of paper. What is the probability that the slip of paper contains the letter G?

    A. $\frac{1}{9}$

    B. $\frac{1}{8}$

    C. $\frac{2}{7}$

    D. $\frac{2}{9}$

Open-Ended Problems

9. In a 50-yard race, the first three finishers were Ed, Peggy, and Val. But you do not know the order in which they finished. Find all the possible ways they could have finished first, second, and third.

10. You are playing a game in which you win if a spinner stops on the number 3. Three spinners are shown below. Which would you choose to use in this game? Explain your answer.

11. Explain how to find the mean and median of a set of 99 numbers.

12. The table below shows the number of home runs Rosario hit from 1995 to 1998. Draw a pictograph that shows Rosario's home runs.

Season	Home Runs
1995	30
1996	25
1997	40
1998	35

CHAPTER *Six*

Algebraic Concepts

Working with number sentences and learning about inverse operations are two examples of algebra that you have seen while studying math. When you reach junior high school or high school, you will spend an entire school year studying algebra as one of your courses. The work you do now helps prepare you for future success in algebra.

Set A: Problems with Strategies

1. What number completes the number sentence?

$$9 + 5 = \Box - 11$$

A. 3 B. 13 C. 15 D. 25

Guess and Check
If you replace the box above with any answer choice, you can check whether that choice is correct or incorrect. Sometimes, multiple-choice problems can be solved that easily. Just keep trying out guesses until you find the correct answer.

STRATEGIES *to Answer the Problem*

YOUR Turn

What number completes the number sentence?

$$8 + 4 = 60 \div \Box$$

A. 5

B. 12

C. 15

D. 48

2. Elijah went to the store with some money. He spent $4 for a pair of socks and $8 for a book. On his way home, he ran into his friend Paula. Paula gave Elijah $6 she owed him. When Elijah got home, he had $10. How much money did Elijah have when he first went to the store?

   A. $28

   B. $18

   C. $16

   D. $4

Work Backward

STRATEGIES *to Answer the Problem*

Sometimes problems can be solved by thinking from the end to the beginning. In this problem, you know how much money Elijah had at the end but you need to find how much he had at the beginning. To work backward, use the fact that addition and subtraction are inverse operations.

YOUR Turn

Find the following number. If you multiply the number by 3 and then add 15 to the product, you get 39. What number is it?

   A. 162

   B. 132

   C. 18

   D. 8

3. Which inequality is true?

   A. $2 + 2 > 2 \times 2$

   B. $2 + 2 < 2 \times 2$

   C. $6 < 0$

   D. $\frac{1}{2} > \frac{1}{3}$

Apply a Rule or Definition

STRATEGIES to Answer the Problem

When you work with inequalities, you must memorize the meanings of the two symbols $<$ and $>$. The symbol $<$ means "is less than" and the symbol $>$ means "is greater than." Reread each inequality above, replacing the symbol with the correct phrase.

YOUR Turn

Which symbol completes the number sentence below?

$$200 - 13 \; \square \; 200 + 13$$

   A. $=$

   B. $>$

   C. $<$

   D. $\times$

4. Bud has 6 dogs. Each dog eats 12 cans of food a week. Which number sentence could you use to find how many cans of food Bud must buy each week?

   A. $6 + 12 = \square$

   B. $12 + 6 = \square$

   C. $6 \times 12 = \square$

   D. $12 \div 6 = \square$

Make a Number Sentence

STRATEGIES *to Answer the Problem*

Before you can solve a word problem, you must understand what it is saying and what it is asking you to find. Then you need to figure out if you can write a number sentence that will help you solve the word problem. Try to picture twelve cans arranged on a table for each of the six dogs. What operation does that remind you of?

YOUR Turn

Prima had nine eggs. She used three of the eggs to make a cake. Which number sentence could be used to find how many eggs Prima has left?

   A. $9 + 3 = \square$

   B. $9 - 3 = \square$

   C. $9 \times 3 = \square$

   D. $9 \div 3 = \square$

5. Jon drew a rectangle. Lee drew a rectangle twice as long and twice as wide as Jon's rectangle. What can you conclude about the areas of the two rectangles?

    A. The area of Lee's rectangle is twice the area of Jon's rectangle.

    B. The area of Lee's rectangle is three times the area of Jon's rectangle.

    C. The area of Lee's rectangle is four times the area of Jon's rectangle.

    D. You cannot form any conclusion about the two areas.

Organize Your Information:
Draw a Picture/Apply a Rule or Definition

STRATEGIES
to Answer the Problem

Area is a measure of the amount of space taken up by a rectangle. To answer this problem, start by drawing a picture of what Jon's rectangle might look like. Then build outward to draw Lee's rectangle twice as long and twice as wide.

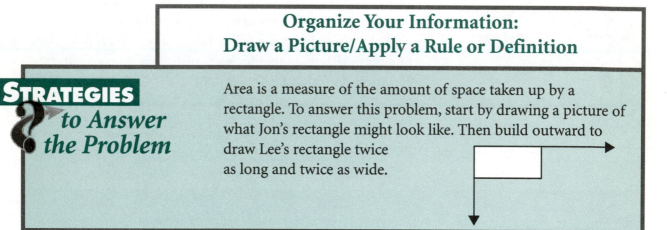

YOUR Turn

Tom's rectangle and Hallie's rectangle have the same length. Tom's rectangle is 1 inch wider than Hallie's. What can you conclude about the perimeters of the two rectangles?

    A. The perimeter of Tom's rectangle is 1 inch greater than the perimeter of Hallie's rectangle.

    B. The perimeter of Tom's rectangle is 2 inches greater than the perimeter of Hallie's rectangle.

    C. The perimeter of Tom's rectangle is 4 inches greater than the perimeter of Hallie's rectangle.

    D. You cannot form any conclusion about the two perimeters.

6. The picture below shows a balanced scale containing square and circular shapes. If a square were added to the left side of the scale, what could you add to the right side to keep the scale balanced?

    A. a circle

    B. a circle and a square

    C. two squares

    D. two circles

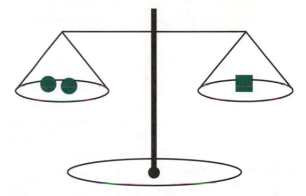

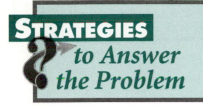
STRATEGIES
to Answer the Problem

Use Manipulatives/ Use Logical Thinking

Work with a scale in your classroom or picture the action taking place. Begin by drawing a new square on the left hand side to show how the scale goes out of balance.

YOUR Turn

In the scale above, what relationship is there between the square and the circle?

    A. The square and the circle have the same weight.

    B. The circle weighs twice as much as the square.

    C. The square weighs twice as much as the circle.

    D. The square weighs three times as much as the circle.

7. Obie is six years older than his brother Stefan. Tawana is four years younger than Obie. Nisha is ten years older than Tawana. Nisha is thirty years old. How old is Stefan?

   A. 16

   B. 18

   C. 22

   D. 24

STRATEGIES
to Answer the Problem

Work Backward/ Use Logical Thinking

When a word problem is complicated, sometimes you can work from one piece of solid information back to the answer you are looking for. In this problem, you are told that Nisha is thirty years old. You can work back from that fact to find Stefan's age, step by step.

YOUR Turn

Larry arrived ten minutes before Renaldo. Jeannette arrived five minutes after Larry. Jane arrived ten minutes before Jeannette. Who arrived first?

   A. Jane

   B. Jeannette

   C. Larry

   D. Renaldo

8. Point **B** lies 2 units to the right of point **A** on a coordinate grid.
Point **A** has coordinates (5, 3). What are the coordinates of point **B**?

A. (7, 3)

B. (5, 5)

C. (5, 1)

D. (3, 3)

Organize Your Information: Make a Chart or Graph

STRATEGIES
to Answer
the Problem

Draw a coordinate grid on graph paper, and locate point **A** at (5, 3). Then find the coordinates of point **B** by counting across.

YOUR Turn

Point **X** has coordinates (2, 2). Point **Y** has coordinates (1, 3). Which diagram below shows how to go from point **X** to point **Y**?

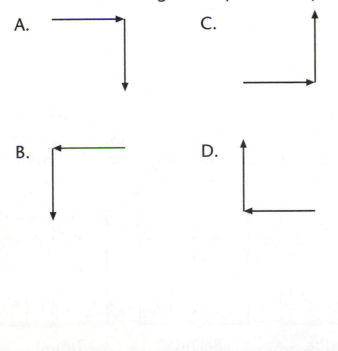

A.

B.

C.

D.

9. The sides of a square are 1 yard long. Twenty copies of this square are placed together in a row to form a rectangle. What is the perimeter of this rectangle?

A. 40 yd.

B. 42 yd.

C. 44 yd.

D. 80 yd.

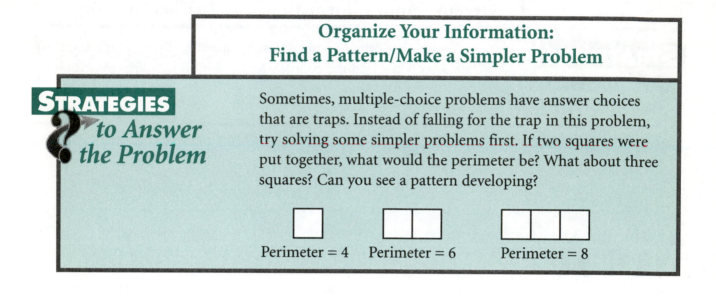

**Organize Your Information:
Find a Pattern/Make a Simpler Problem**

STRATEGIES *to Answer the Problem*

Sometimes, multiple-choice problems have answer choices that are traps. Instead of falling for the trap in this problem, try solving some simpler problems first. If two squares were put together, what would the perimeter be? What about three squares? Can you see a pattern developing?

Perimeter = 4   Perimeter = 6   Perimeter = 8

YOUR Turn

Rhonda formed 2 sections by folding a sheet of paper in half once. Belinda formed 4 sections by folding a piece of paper in half two times. Timothy formed 16 sections by folding a sheet of paper in half. How many times did Timothy fold his sheet in half?

A. 4

B. 6

C. 8

D. 10

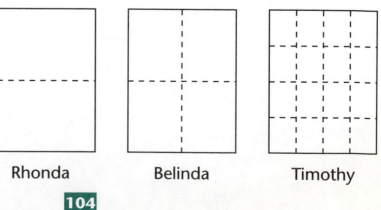

Rhonda   Belinda   Timothy

Set B: Practice Problems

Enhanced Multiple-Choice

1. Vicky was thinking of a number. She multiplied the number by 2 and then added 8 to the product. The number she then had was 20. What number was she originally thinking of?

   A. 6   B. 24   C. 48   D. 56

2. Point **A** has coordinates (6, 7). Point **B** has coordinates (7, 6). Which diagram below shows how to go from point **A** to point **B**?

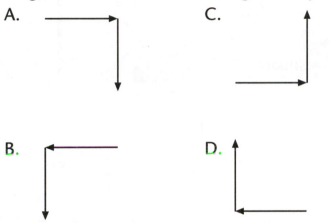

   A.

   C.

   B.

   D.

3. On Monday, Sharon told the class, "My birthday is 7 weeks from tomorrow." How many days away is Sharon's birthday?

   A. 8

   B. 36

   C. 43

   D. 50

4. What number completes the number sentence?

   $$11 + 4 - 6 = 5 + \square$$

   A. 4

   B. 5

   C. 6

   D. 8

5. Which symbol completes the number sentence?

$$4 + 5 \,\square\, 4 \times 5$$

A. $=$

B. $<$

C. $>$

D. $\div$

6. The picture below shows a balanced scale containing square shapes, circular shapes, and triangular shapes. If a triangle were added to the right side of the scale, what could you add to the left side to keep the scale balanced?

A. one square

B. two squares

C. a circle and a square

D. two circles

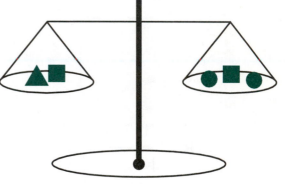

7. Point **W** lies 4 units above point **T** on a coordinate grid. Point **W** has coordinates (8, 6). What are the coordinates of point **T**?

A. (4, 6)

B. (8, 2)

C. (8, 10)

D. (12, 6)

8. Alex has twice as many pennies as Cynthia. Darryl has 4 more pennies than Cynthia. Darryl has 9 pennies. How many pennies does Alex have?

A. 26

B. 13

C. 10

D. 5

Open-Ended Problems

9. Ask three people their ages. Then write a number sentence that uses those three numbers.

10. Draw a coordinate plane. Then find two points that are exactly two units from the point (4, 6).

11. Find three different numbers that make this inequality false.

$$100 + 20 > 10 \times \Box$$

12. A triangle weighs twice as much as a square. A circle weighs twice as much as a triangle. Draw a balanced scale that holds triangles, squares, and circles.

Set C: Chapter Test
Enhanced Multiple-Choice

1. Hubert has 64 baseball cards. Each page of his album can hold 4 cards. Hubert wants to know how many pages he will fill with his baseball cards. Which number sentence could Hubert use to find this number?
   A. $64 + 4 = \square$
   B. $64 - 4 = \square$
   C. $64 \times 4 = \square$
   D. $64 \div 4 = \square$

2. A rectangle has a perimeter of 48 feet. The length of each side of the rectangle is increased by 5 feet. How does the perimeter of the rectangle change?
   A. The perimeter increases by 5 ft.
   B. The perimeter increases by 10 ft.
   C. The perimeter increases by 20 ft.
   D. The perimeter increases by 25 ft.

3. Which number sentence is true?
   A. $7 + 7 = 7 \times 7$
   B. $5 + 4 < 5 + 4 - 3$
   C. $3 \times 0 < 3 + 0$
   D. $3 + 1 < 3 \times 1$

4. The picture below shows a balanced scale containing square shapes, circular shapes, and triangular shapes. Which figures have the same weight?
   A. the circle and the triangle
   B. the circle and the square
   C. the triangle and the square
   D. the circle and the hexagon

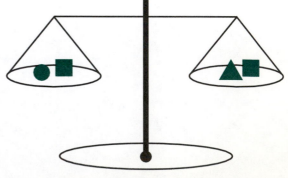

5. Aaron, Bea, Charli, and Dan ran a race. Bea finished ahead of Charli. Dan finished behind Aaron. Aaron finished ahead of Bea. Who finished the race first?

A.   Aaron

B.   Bea

C.   Charli

D.   Dan

6. What number completes the number sentence?

$$8 \times 5 = 80 \div \square$$

A.   1

B.   2

C.   3

D.   4

7. What is the area of the rectangle below?

A.   16 sq cm

B.   32 sq cm

C.   54 sq cm

D.   63 sq cm

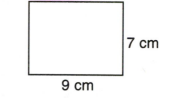

7 cm

9 cm

8. What number makes both inequalities true?

$$6 + \square > 7$$

$$6 \times \square > 18$$

A.   1

B.   2

C.   3

D.   4

Open-Ended Problems

9. Find three different numbers that make the inequality true.

$$5 + 6 < 3 + \square$$

10. The scale below is balanced. Explain how the weight of a triangle is related to the weight of a square.

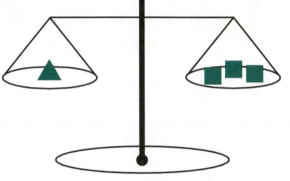

11. Find the length and width of three different rectangles that have an area of 24 square feet.

12. The five points on the coordinate grid below all lie on a line. Identify the coordinates of each point. Then describe any patterns you see in the coordinates.

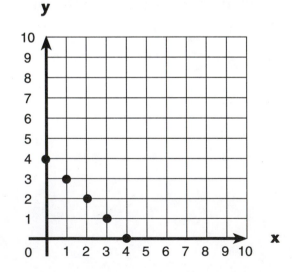

Unit 3 Practice Tests

Introduction

Here are two full-length practice tests. These tests are similar to the standardized math tests you may take in school. Each practice test is divided into three sections as follows:

- **Part 1** contains 50 multiple-choice questions. Selecting the correct answer from four choices is what is most important in this part. You do not need to show your work in this section.

- **Part 2** contains 5 short-answer problems. Here you will need to figure out the correct answer on your own as there are no choices, but you do not need to show your work.

- **Part 3** contains 5 open-ended questions. You must show your work when answering these questions. Even if you do not get the correct answer, you can still get some credit if your work makes sense.

Practice Test A

Directions for Math Practice Test A, Part 1

Work each problem and select the best answer.

1. What number is missing from the sequence below?

4, 11, 18, ☐, 32, 39, …

A. 19

B. 22

C. 25

D. 28

2. What is the figure below called?

A. hexagon

B. octagon

C. pentagon

D. trapezoid

3. Which number is greatest?

A. 8.73

B. 8.089

C. 8.8

D. 7.98

4. Which number completes the number sentence correctly?

$6 \times 8 = ☐ + 10$

A. 4

B. 38

C. 47

D. 48

5. A number cube contains the numbers 1, 2, 3, 4, 5, and 6. The number cube is rolled once. What is the probability that the number 5 is rolled?

A. $\frac{1}{6}$

B. $\frac{1}{5}$

C. $\frac{5}{1}$

D. $\frac{5}{6}$

6. What fraction of the circles is shaded?

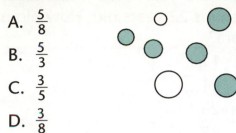

A. $\frac{5}{8}$

B. $\frac{5}{3}$

C. $\frac{3}{5}$

D. $\frac{3}{8}$

7. Ursula's batting average was 0.356. What digit is in the tenths place of Ursula's batting average?

A. 0

B. 3

C. 5

D. 6

8. What is the perimeter of the square?

A. 14 m

B. 28 m

C. 49 m

D. 98 m

7 m

9. Pia has 9 boxes. Each box holds 8 books. How many books does Pia have in all?

A. 17

B. 64

C. 72

D. 81

10. A recipe requires 2 cups of flour to make 24 biscuits. How many cups of flour do you need to make 72 biscuits?

A. 4

B. 5

C. 6

D. 7

GO ON

Rene bowled 9 times last month. Her scores are shown in the table below. Use the table to answer problems 11-13.

Game	1	2	3	4	5	6	7	8	9
Score	98	104	122	100	111	112	136	127	125

11. What was Rene's mean score?
A. 111
B. 112
C. 113
D. 115

12. What was Rene's median score?
A. 111
B. 112
C. 113
D. 115

13. What was the range of Rene's scores?
A. 136
B. 68
C. 38
D. 27

14. Tara is 6 years older than Kate. Kate is 5 years older than Reed. Reed is 22 years old. How old is Tara?
A. 11
B. 21
C. 23
D. 33

15. What is the difference?
$$53.4 - 2.71 = \square$$
A. 26.3
B. 36.3
C. 50.69
D. 51.69

GO ON

16. A school held elections for student president. The circle graph shows the results of the election. Who got the greatest number of votes?

Voting Results for School President

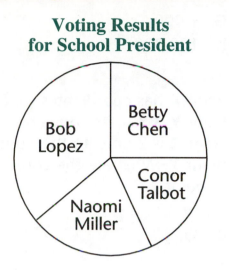

A. Betty Chen
B. Bob Lopez
C. Naomi Miller
D. Conor Talbot

17. Valerie bought a loaf of bread for $2.19 and a jar of peanut butter for $2.89. She paid the cashier with a $20 bill. About how much change did Valerie get?

A. $5
B. $6
C. $15
D. $16

18. Which symbol completes the number sentence?

$$6 + 0 \ \square \ 6$$

A. <
B. >
C. +
D. =

19. Which figure must contain perpendicular sides?

A. parallelogram
B. trapezoid
C. rectangle
D. octagon

20. Mallory has $1.75 in nickels. How many nickels does Mallory have?

A. 35
B. 33
C. 31
D. 15

21. Which angle is acute?

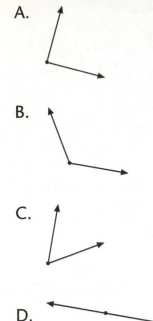

A.

B.

C.

D.

22. Louis bought 36 bagels. Some were plain bagels and some were garlic bagels. Louis bought twice as many plain bagels as garlic bagels. How many garlic bagels did Louis buy?

A. 24
B. 16
C. 14
D. 12

23. How many centimeters are there in 1 meter?

A. 10
B. 100
C. 1,000
D. 100,000

24. Point **X** has coordinates (6, 8). Point **Y** is 3 units above point **X**. Point **Z** is 2 units to the right of point **Y**. What are the coordinates of point **Z**?

A. (9, 6)
B. (9, 10)
C. (8, 5)
D. (8, 11)

25. Find a number between 50 and 100. The sum of its digits is 13. The number is a multiple of 5. What is the number?

A. 76
B. 80
C. 85
D. 175

26. How long is the telephone, including the antenna, measured to the nearest inch?

A. 5

B. $4\frac{1}{2}$

C. 4

D. 12

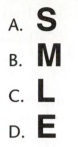

27. How is the number 280.7 written in words?

A. two hundred and eighty-seven tenths

B. two hundred eighty and seven tenths

C. two hundred and eighty-seven hundredths

D. two hundred eighty and seven hundredths

28. Which letter has a vertical line of symmetry?

A. **S**

B. **M**

C. **L**

D. **E**

29. An eraser weighs twice as much as a pen. A pen weighs three times as much as a piece of chalk. How are the weights of an eraser and a piece of chalk related?

A. An eraser weighs six times as much as a piece of chalk.

B. An eraser weighs five times as much as a piece of chalk.

C. A piece of chalk weighs six times as much as an eraser.

D. A piece of chalk weighs five times as much as an eraser.

30. Nikki worked 7 hours yesterday and earned $98. How much did Nikki earn per hour?

A. $9.10

B. $11

C. $13

D. $14

31. Todd drew two rectangles. His second rectangle was 5 inches longer and 5 inches wider than his first rectangle. What can you conclude about the areas of his two rectangles?

A. The area of the second rectangle is 5 square inches greater than the area of the first rectangle.

B. The area of the second rectangle is 10 square inches greater than the area of the first rectangle.

C. The area of the second rectangle is 25 square inches greater than the area of the first rectangle.

D. You cannot form any conclusion about the areas of the two rectangles.

32. Sixty students signed up for basketball tryouts. The coach divided the students into teams with five players on each team. Which number sentence could be used to find the number of teams the coach formed?

A. $60 + 5 = \square$

B. $60 - 5 = \square$

C. $60 \times 5 = \square$

D. $60 \div 5 = \square$

33. The table below shows input and output. What rule can you use to convert input to output?

Input	Output
4	24
5	30
6	36
7	42

A. add 20

B. subtract 20

C. divide by 6

D. multiply by 6

34. What number sentence can you use to find the number of circles in the diagram below?

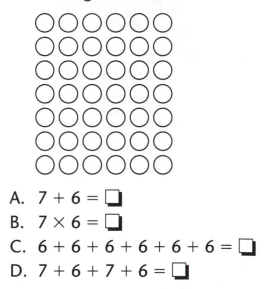

A. $7 + 6 = \square$

B. $7 \times 6 = \square$

C. $6 + 6 + 6 + 6 + 6 + 6 = \square$

D. $7 + 6 + 7 + 6 = \square$

35. A snail crawled $\frac{1}{2}$ inch on Monday and $\frac{1}{4}$ inch on Tuesday. How far did the snail crawl in all?

A. $\frac{1}{8}$ in. C. $\frac{2}{6}$ in.

B. $\frac{2}{8}$ in. D. $\frac{3}{4}$ in.

36. The spinner shown below is spun twice. Which of the following is impossible?

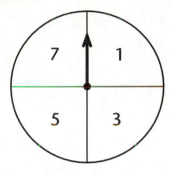

A. Both spins land on the number 1.

B. The sum of the two spins is an even number.

C. The sum of the two spins is an odd number.

D. The sum of the two spins is greater than 10.

37. Silvio left home with some money in his pocket. He spent $1.50 for a bus ride to town, $4 for lunch, $6 for a movie, and $1.50 for a bus ride home. When he got home, he had $24 left. How much money did he have when he first left home?

A. $11

B. $36

C. $37

D. $38

38. Which of the following is the best way to estimate 42 × 98?

A. 40 × 90

B. 50 × 90

C. 40 × 100

D. 50 × 100

39. Leah has 24 roses. One-fourth of her roses are white. How many of Leah's roses are white?

A. 4

B. 6

C. 8

D. 12

40. How is the number 9,670 written in expanded form?

A. (9 × 1,000) + (6 × 100) + (7 × 10)

B. (9 × 1,000) + (6 × 100) + (7 × 1)

C. (9 × 10,000) + (6 × 100) + (7 × 10)

D. (9 × 100) + (6 × 10) + (7 × 1)

GO ON

41. What shape comes next in the pattern?

○□△○○○○□△○○○

A. ○

B. □

C. △

D. ○

42. Hu has quarters, dimes, and nickels. He has nine coins in all. He has at least one of each type of coin. What is the greatest amount of money Hu could have in his pocket?

A. $1.20

B. $1.90

C. $2.25

D. $2.40

43. Three students measured their heights and filled in the table below. How are the students ordered from tallest to shortest?

Student	Height
Boris	52 in.
Cara	4 ft. 5 in.
Ed	1 yd. 1 ft.

A. Cara, Boris, Ed

B. Cara, Ed, Boris

C. Ed, Boris, Cara

D. Ed, Cara, Boris

44. Flo did 70 sit-ups each day for 42 consecutive days. About how many sit-ups did Flo do in all?

A. 100

B. 300

C. 3,000

D. 30,000

45. Javier rode his bicycle 1 block north, then 2 blocks east, then 3 blocks south, and then 4 blocks west. Where was Javier when he finished riding?

A. 1 block south and 1 block west of where he started

B. 2 blocks south and 2 blocks west of where he started

C. 3 blocks south and 3 blocks west of where he started

D. 4 blocks south and 6 blocks west of where he started

46. The population of a town is shown in the table below for the years 1970, 1980, and 1990.

Year	Population
1970	5,870
1980	6,236
1990	6,749

By how many people did the population increase between 1980 and 1990?

A. 366

B. 513

C. 879

D. 979

47. Which number is a mixed number?

A. $\frac{1}{3}$

B. 2.4

C. $3\frac{1}{7}$

D. $\frac{11}{5}$

48. How many whole numbers between 1 and 50 have no remainder when divided by 7?

A. 6

B. 7

C. 8

D. 43

The bar graph shows the price of a newspaper over five years. Use the bar graph to answer problems 49 and 50.

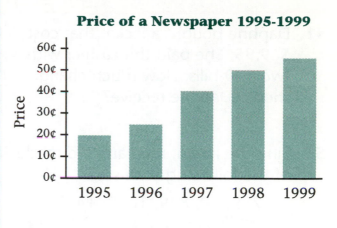

Price of a Newspaper 1995-1999

49. What was the price of a newspaper in 1995?

A. 2 cents

B. 10 cents

C. 20 cents

D. 25 cents

50. Between which years did the price of a newspaper increase by the greatest amount?

A. 1995 and 1996

B. 1996 and 1997

C. 1997 and 1998

D. 1998 and 1999

Directions for Math Practice Test A, Part 2

Solve each problem. You do not need to show your work. You just need to show the answer.

51. Daphne bought a jacket that cost $69.95. She paid the cashier with two $50 bills. How much change should Daphne receive?

52. Find the mean, median, and mode of the following data set:

7, 9, 10, 8, 9, 10, 7, 14, 7

53. Find the area and perimeter of the rectangle.

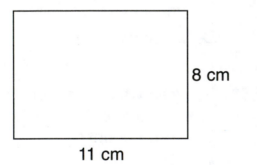

8 cm

11 cm

54. Todd is twice as old as his sister Regina. Their father is twice as old as Todd. Todd is 28 years old. How old are their father and Regina?

55. Find the next three terms in the sequence.

4, 13, 22, 31, ...

Directions for Math Practice Test A, Part 3

Give complete answers to all parts of the five problems that follow. Show all your work.

56. Cassie had 16 cookies. She gave $\frac{1}{4}$ of them to a friend. Draw a picture that shows how to find $\frac{1}{4}$ of 16.

57. Explain how millimeters, centimeters, meters, and kilometers are related.

58. Each circle below represents the number 1. The shaded parts shown represent a number. Explain how to express the shaded parts as a fraction and as a mixed number.

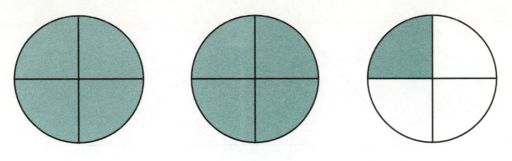

 GO ON

59. Explain what it means for figures to be similar. Then draw a triangle similar to the one shown.

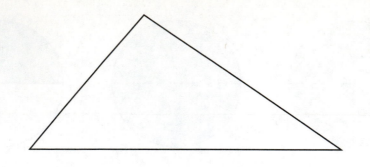

60. The table below shows twenty students' choices of their favorite color. Draw a graph that fits the data.

Color	Number of Students
red	8
blue	6
green	4
purple	2

Practice Test B

Directions for Math Practice Test B, Part 1

Work each problem and select the best answer.

1. What is the sum?

2.41 + 3.13 + 2.7

A. 8.24

B. 7.24

C. 5.81

D. 5.71

2. Which number sentence is false?

A. $189 \times 1 > 189 + 1$

B. $\frac{1}{5} < \frac{1}{4}$

C. $7 \times 0 = 0$

D. $100 \div 10 = 10$

3. Jennifer made 36 brownies for a party. Twelve people were at the party. Jennifer wants to give each of the twelve people the same number of brownies. How many brownies can she give each person?

A. 2

B. 3

C. 4

D. 24

4. Four students went bird-watching and kept track of how many different kinds of birds they spotted. The pictograph shows what they found.

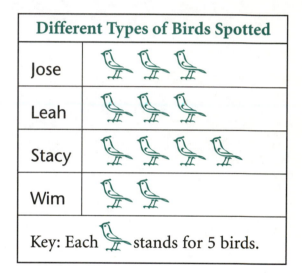

Different Types of Birds Spotted

Key: Each 🐦 stands for 5 birds.

How many different types of birds did Stacy spot?

A. 4

B. 10

C. 15

D. 20

5. Sal drove 289 miles in 6 hours. How fast did Sal drive, rounded to the nearest 10 miles per hour?

A. 30

B. 40

C. 50

D. 60

6. A bag contains 10 slips of paper. The letters H, O, D, G, E, P, O, D, G, E are written on one slip of paper each. Paul reaches into the bag and selects a slip of paper. What is the probability that the slip of paper contains a vowel?

   A. $\frac{5}{26}$

   B. $\frac{1}{10}$

   C. $\frac{3}{10}$

   D. $\frac{2}{5}$

7. Which fraction is greatest?

   A. $\frac{1}{2}$

   B. $\frac{1}{5}$

   C. $\frac{2}{5}$

   D. $\frac{1}{10}$

8. Bart has $8 in dimes. How many dimes does Bart have?

   A. 8

   B. 80

   C. 800

   D. 8,000

9. What number is missing from the sequence below?

$$2, 6, 18, \square, 162, \ldots$$

   A. 22

   B. 30

   C. 44

   D. 54

10. What number makes both inequalities true?

$$8 + \square > 10$$
$$8 \times \square < 32$$

   A. 0

   B. 2

   C. 3

   D. 5

GO ON

11. Students were asked to do volunteer work one Saturday. The number of boys and the number of girls from grades 3-6 who volunteered are shown in the table below. Which grade had the greatest number of volunteers?

Grade	Boys	Girls
3	15	24
4	19	18
5	20	15
6	14	20

A. 3
B. 4
C. 5
D. 6

12. Which unit is most appropriate for measuring the height of a tall office building?
A. millimeter
B. centimeter
C. meter
D. kilometer

13. Find a number between 10 and 60. The number is a multiple of 7. The number is also a multiple of 6. What is the number?
A. 84
B. 49
C. 42
D. 13

14. Fran's birthday is on a Tuesday. Theo's birthday is 40 days later. On what day of the week does Theo's birthday fall?
A. Monday
B. Thursday
C. Saturday
D. Sunday

15. The price of a candy bar is shown in the table below for four different years.

Year	Price
1965	5 cents
1970	8 cents
1980	25 cents
1999	60 cents

By how much did the price of a candy bar increase between 1970 and 1999?
A. 35 cents
B. 52 cents
C. 55 cents
D. 60 cents

GO ON

16. In this figure, all sides must have the same length. What figure could it be?

A. rectangle

B. square

C. trapezoid

D. triangle

17. The picture below shows a balanced scale containing square and triangular shapes. If a triangle were added to the right side of the scale, what could you add to the left side to keep the scale balanced?

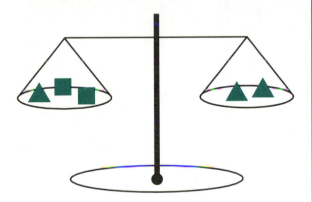

A. a square

B. two squares

C. a square and a triangle

D. two triangles

18. Lance paid for two ties with a $50 bill. One tie cost $12.99 and the other tie cost $16.99. Which of the following is the best estimate of the change Lance should have received?

A. $20

B. $21

C. $22

D. $30

19. How far is it from Sulphur Springs to Morgans Creek?

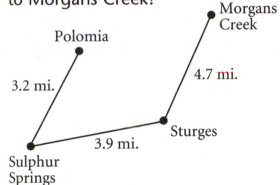

A. 11.8 mi.

B. 10.8 mi.

C. 8.6 mi.

D. 7.6 mi.

20. What letter comes next in the pattern below?

H, I, H, O, H, I, H, O, ____

A. H

B. I

C. O

D. U

21. What fraction of the square is shaded?

A. $\frac{1}{4}$

B. $\frac{1}{3}$

C. $\frac{3}{1}$

D. $\frac{4}{1}$

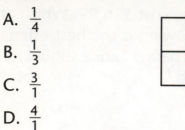

Use the line graph to answer problems 22-23.

Membership in the Cooking Club

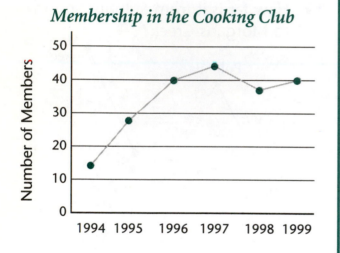

22. About how many members were there in 1995?

A. 50

B. 40

C. 30

D. 20

23. In which year was the greatest membership?

A. 1999

B. 1998

C. 1997

D. 1996

24. Iris is thinking of a number. She multiplies the number by 2 and then adds 6 to the product. The result is 40. What number was she originally thinking of?

A. 14

B. 17

C. 86

D. 92

25. Which fraction is **not** equivalent to $\frac{1}{6}$?

A. $\frac{2}{12}$

B. $\frac{10}{60}$

C. $\frac{3}{20}$

D. $\frac{4}{24}$

26. Simone gave $\frac{1}{2}$ of her allowance to her brother. Her allowance was $8. How much did she give her brother?

A. $2.00

B. $2.80

C. $3.00

D. $4.00

27. How is the number $(4 \times 1,000) + (2 \times 10) + (5 \times 1)$ written in standard form?

A. 425

B. 4,025

C. 4,205

D. 4,250

28. The length of each side of a square is increased by 3 inches. How does the perimeter of the square change?

A. The perimeter increases by 3 inches.

B. The perimeter increases by 6 inches.

C. The perimeter increases by 12 inches.

D. There is not enough information to tell how the perimeter changes.

29. Which number is even?

A. 2.2

B. 10

C. 8,881

D. 9,999

30. Belle started work at the time shown on the first clock. She finished work at the time shown on the second clock. How long did Belle work?

Belle started work

Belle finished work

A. 4 hr. 45 min.

B. 5 hr. 15 min.

C. 5 hr. 45 min.

D. 7 hr. 15 min.

31. In the table below, input is converted to output using a certain rule. What output should go in the empty space?

Input	Output
1	22
3	24
5	26
7	

A. 8
B. 9
C. 27
D. 28

32. Oscar played golf six times last month. He added his six scores together and divided the sum by 6. What did Oscar compute?

A. his mean
B. his median
C. his mode
D. his range

33. The cost of mailing a letter is 33 cents if the letter weighs 1 ounce or less. If the letter weighs more than 1 ounce, the cost is 33 cents for the first ounce and 22 cents for each extra ounce. How much would it cost to mail a letter weighing 4 ounces?

A. $1.32
B. $1.21
C. $1.11
D. $0.99

34. Which number completes the number sentence correctly?

$$6 + 18 = 30 - \square$$

A. 54
B. 18
C. 16
D. 6

35. How many faces does the pyramid have?

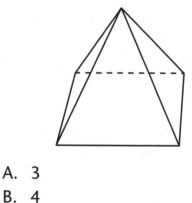

A. 3
B. 4
C. 5
D. 8

GO ON

36. The numbers 1, 2, 3, 4, 5, and 6 are written on the six faces of a number cube. The number cube is rolled 300 times. About how many times would you expect the number 6 to appear?

A. 50

B. 60

C. 100

D. 150

37. The temperatures at 8 A.M. and 2 P.M. are shown on the thermometers below. How much colder was it at 8 A.M. than at 2 P.M.?

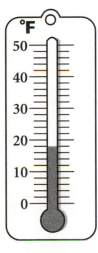
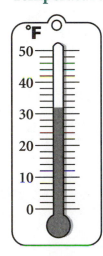

A. 7° F

B. 14° F

C. 16° F

D. 24° F

38. How is the number *seventy-seven and eight tenths* written in standard form?

A. 70.78

B. 77.08

C. 77.78

D. 77.8

39. A bus can hold 40 people. There are 192 people going on a school bus trip. How many buses will be needed?

A. 4

B. 5

C. 6

D. 8

40. Tee shirts are being sold at Jake's school. Red tee shirts and blue tee shirts are sold in small, medium, large, and extra large sizes. How many different types of tee shirts are there?

A. 4

B. 6

C. 8

D. 16

41. How many circles will there be in the sixth figure of the pattern?

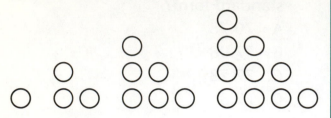

    A. 14

    B. 15

    C. 20

    D. 21

42. Which of the following is **not** equivalent to 5×4?

    A. $5 + 5 + 5 + 5$

    B. $4 + 4 + 4 + 4 + 4$

    C. 4×5

    D. $5 \times 1 \times 1 \times 1 \times 1$

43. What are the coordinates of point **A**?

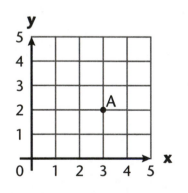

    A. (2, 2)

    B. (2, 3)

    C. (3, 3)

    D. (3, 2)

44. There are 40 girls and boys in a theater group. There are six more girls than boys. How many girls are there in the theater group?

    A. 26

    B. 23

    C. 17

    D. 14

45. There were 4,120 people at a basketball game. Of these, 1,856 paid less than full price for their tickets. How many paid full price for their tickets?

    A. 2,264

    B. 2,364

    C. 3,264

    D. 5,976

46. The perimeter of a rectangle is 20 feet and its area is 24 square feet. What are the length and width of the rectangle?

A. 8 ft. and 3 ft.

B. 8 ft. and 2 ft.

C. 6 ft. and 4 ft.

D. 5 ft. and 5 ft.

47. Which fraction is equivalent to $\frac{3}{4}$?

A. $\frac{2}{3}$

B. $\frac{30}{40}$

C. $\frac{32}{42}$

D. $\frac{12}{15}$

48. Charlene has four coins in her pocket. Their total value is fifty cents. How many nickels does Charlene have in her pocket?

A. 0

B. 1

C. 2

D. 3

49. Points **A** and **B** lie on a coordinate grid. Point **A** has coordinates (0, 5). Point **B** has coordinates (5, 0). Which diagram below shows how to go from point **A** to point **B**?

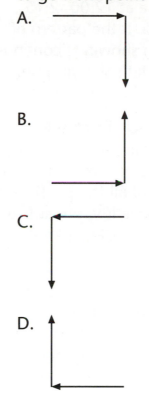

A.

B.

C.

D.

50. An hour contains 60 minutes and a day contains 24 hours. How many minutes are there in 1 day?

A. 84

B. 144

C. 1,240

D. 1,440

Directions for Math Practice Test B, Part 2

Solve each problem. You do not need to show your work. You just need to show the answer.

51. The first four showings of a movie in a theater are at 12:00, 2:15, 4:30, and 6:45. If the pattern of times between showings continues, when will the fifth showing be?

52. MaryAnn's Lunch Truck sells vanilla, chocolate, and strawberry milkshakes in small, medium, and large sizes. Find all the possible choices you have if you want to buy a milkshake at MaryAnn's.

53. Carol had a library book due on April 10, but she returned it late. There is a charge of $0.20 for every day a book is late. Carol owed $1.80 on her book. On what date did Carol return her book?

54. Points **T** and **W** lie on a coordinate grid. Point **W** has coordinates (6, 3). Point **T** lies 2 units above point **W** and 3 units to the left of point **W**. What are the coordinates of point **T**?

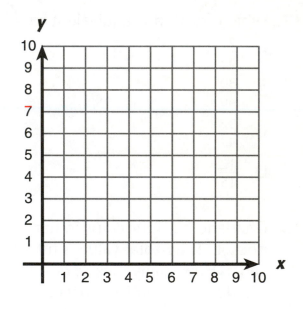

55. How many pints are there in 1 gallon?

Directions for Math Practice Test B, Part 3

Give complete answers to all parts of the five problems that follow. Show all your work.

56. Explain how you would estimate the product 98 × 14.

57. Name three different types of polygons that contain parallel sides. Draw an example of each type.

GO ON

58. The table below shows one input and its output. Find a rule that could be used to create the output from the input. Then use your rule to complete the table.

Input	Output
4	8
5	
6	
7	
8	

59. Create a set of five numbers that has a mean of 20 and a range of 10.

60. A square drawn on a coordinate grid has one corner at (3, 3). Complete the square and identify the coordinates of its three other corners.